COLLEGE ABROAD

HOW TO GET AN INTERNATIONAL EDUCATION, A DEGREE, AND A NEW PERSPECTIVE ON LIFE AND THE WORLD

HOLLY OBERLE

College Abroad

International Standard Book Number: 978-0-9721328-9-3
Library of Congress Catalog Card Number: 2012955700

Agapy LLC
Charleston, IL
Website: www.agapy.com

Printed in the United States of America

To Mom and Dad, who hated to see me go away, but always had a plane ticket ready for me to come home.

About the Author

Holly Oberle grew up in Fort Collins, Colorado. She holds a B.A. in International Relations and Women's Studies from Knox College in Galesburg, Illinois and an M.A. in International Relations and Social Theory from Jacobs University and Bremen Universität in Germany. She completed a Doctoral Fellowship at the Hebrew University in Jerusalem and is a PhD candidate at the Berlin Graduate School for Transnational Studies. She researches feminist theory of language and gender in foreign policy, and is expected to complete her doctorate in 2013. In addition to Israel, Germany and the United States, she has also lived and studied in Budapest, Hungary.

Besides traveling as much as possible, Holly is an animal lover, enjoys vegetarian cooking, swimming, jogging, and listening to Beethoven.

Contents

Preface

> "...Saying 'yes' begins things. Saying 'yes' is how things grow. Saying 'yes' leads to knowledge. 'Yes' is for young people. So for as long as you have the strength to, say 'yes.'" —Stephen Colbert

As I begin writing this book, I sit on a train from Berlin to Budapest. Since moving to Europe, trains have become my main mode of transportation. When traveling by train, the world appears to be passing you by, but when the train stops almost magically in a new time and place, it is suddenly clear that both you and the world have sojourned together. College is the same way. It is the vehicle through which many young people leave the familiarity of home, bring their perspectives to bear on the world, and allow the world to change them as well.

I left my home in northern Colorado to attend Knox College in rural Galesburg, Illinois. After earning a bachelor's degree, I started job hunting, not knowing what I wanted or where I was heading. I ended up accepting a position in Chicago. It felt good for a while, moving forward on the prescribed path for happiness: succeed in high school in order to get into a good college, succeed in college to find a good job, succeed in the job market and have a nice life.

But then one day I wondered if my journey was really complete. I remember sitting in my Chicago high-rise office, reminiscing about my college experience. The next thing I did was return to my college campus to attend the graduation of my younger friends, meet up with former professors, and seek the inspiration I had once felt as a student. The graduation speaker was an uncommon choice. Stephen Colbert made the speech almost entirely in character, but, in what has become the brilliance of his humor, there was a moment when Colbert the person and Colbert the television character became indistinct. He was describing a lesson he learned in his early days as an improv comedian: good actors take the script given to them by the other actors, accept the premise, and further develop the story. Colbert described this process as "yes-anding" as in "*yes,* we're stranded on a deserted island, *and* we've discovered an alien-human hybrid species from the future that provides endless supplies of ice cream!" Later, sitting again in my Chicago high-rise, it struck me that life is either a script we simply follow or a journey we write ourselves.

When I realized that I was merely following a pre-written script for happiness, and saying "no" to my own journey, I decided to change. I put away the script and started to pen my own story. I wanted to see the world, learn about different cultures, further my education, master another language, and meet new people. I could have studied abroad as an undergraduate student in Germany, but instead, I had said "no" and was full of regret. So, I started researching graduate schools in Germany. I found one program that looked attractive, and then I went through a bout of fear. That is really what saying "no" to anything is all about—fear. I feared leaving my job, I feared leaving Chicago, I feared going back to school, I feared the language barrier, I feared school would be more difficult, and I feared they would turn around and say "no." But I pushed through all this trepidation and sent the application anyway. And guess what? They said "yes!" But I didn't "yes-and" back. Instead, I let my fears overwhelm me and said "no."

Again, I regretted my decision and a year later I reapplied. But this time, *they* said "no." It was devastating, but in some ways I shouldn't have been surprised. "Yeses" beget more "yeses," and "no's" beget "no's." So, instead of admitting defeat, I applied to some other programs—all of them abroad. And within a few weeks of applying, I was hearing multiple yeses. That is how I made my life into a real journey—a journey that has now taken me to 32 countries, and has resulted in a master's degree. I said "yes" to a program in Germany, "yes" to living abroad, "yes" to learning a foreign language, "yes" to furthering my education, and "yes" to meeting new and interesting people. Those yeses eventually led me to a PhD program in Germany. And that yes led me to living in Hungary and Israel for a time. Being in a PhD program allowed me also to travel to a number of locations for conferences and field research—places like Japan and Iceland. And it led me to write this book. And I hope this book leads you to say "yes, and" as well, to put away the script and begin your journey.

1. Why College Abroad?

"A desk is a dangerous place from which to view the world." —John le Carré

With the economy continuing to flounder, there is lots of talk about the declining value of higher education. Indeed, getting a degree is no longer a guarantee of getting a job. While the cost of education has increased exponentially, the average income remains stagnant. Personal growth and fulfillment are important elements of a college experience, but paying tens of thousands of dollars for it doesn't always feel like a smart financial decision.

There is nothing wrong with avoiding college and embarking on a different path. However, the fact remains that most employers require at least a bachelor's degree or commensurate experience. While avoiding the high costs of college may sound good on the surface, a recent study conducted by the United States Census Bureau estimates that every degree you get beyond high school is worth around $1 million *each* in additional lifetime income.

Still, education isn't *all* about money. You might have heard about all the experience and wisdom you can attain from traveling. Learning a new language, interacting with another culture, visiting the actual places you read about in your history class—perhaps you can learn and grow by taking a year off between high school and college, and doing a round-the-world "gap" year. In fact, this is normal in some parts of the world. While traveling abroad will undoubtedly change a person for the better, translating a year of aimless travel into experience akin to a college degree is rather difficult. Unless you really gain something during your gap year that is resume-worthy, like becoming fluent in a foreign language or having done significant work abroad, it cannot replace a degree.

It seems as if young Americans are facing a very different world than their parents faced. Everything is less certain than it was only a generation ago. There is pressure to do the "right" thing and get a degree, but also to take advantage of youth, see the world, be adventurous, and do things differently than those before. Fortunately, there is a way to do both: enroll directly, full-time in a college *abroad*.

While this may seem like a radical idea, consider the fact that students all over the world are embarking on this journey without much hesitation. According to an independent article written by a statistician of the *Times Higher Education* (an organization that ranks global universities), 3.3 million students a year are studying outside their home country. In 2009, around 115,000 (6.15%) German students were pursuing a degree outside of Germany, and a stunning 440,000 Chinese students, according to the German *Statistisches Bundesamt*, and UNESCO, respectively. Compare this to only 43,000 (0.3%) American students, according to the Institute of International Education.

Looking back at my classmates in Germany, I can positively say that I was the ONLY one who had not studied in a foreign country before. My roommate and best friend was from the isolated country of Turkmenistan, and yet she was able to complete her bachelor's degree between the United States and Kyrgyzstan, and finally a master's in Germany. I was also the only one who was monolingual. My classmates spoke English and their native tongues fluently, and most had at least working knowledge of a third and fourth language.

College abroad, polyglotism, moving overseas on your own—these are things that young people outside the United States are doing en masse. Even so, according to the Institute of International Education less than 2% of American students are studying abroad, let alone going abroad for college full-time. When Americans do study abroad, most of them go for *less than eight weeks* in what is usually a highly structured environment. While this experience may be valuable for American students, it does not compare with the experience that international students are getting. It is these international students with whom you will be competing in the job market—students who have developed more independence, international experience, language skills, and cultural competence than most American graduates.

American universities know this, which is why they sell themselves the way they do. They tell you that attending their institution will not only get you a competitive degree, but will provide you with an unparalleled *experience*. Their brochures are filled with pictures of happy and curious groups of students discussing hot topics, attending sporting events, and participating in cultural activities. They emphasize their international student population, their extensive study-abroad opportunities, and how much they value learning both in and outside of the classroom. Then they try to show you that theirs is a place of limitless opportunities where you can truly find yourself. Ironically, living and studying in a foreign country naturally provide what America's most liberal universities are trying to sell.

There are also practical advantages to going to college in another country. First, you may be able to complete a degree in less time than you otherwise would in the United States. This means more time for job hunting, traveling, and volunteering. You may be able to get a higher quality education for much less money, or *free*! Living abroad is also the fastest and easiest way to learn a foreign language, which looks good on anyone's resume. Finally, traveling and seeing more of the world can be easier and more cost effective from your international location. In effect, you'll be getting two educations: what you learn in the classroom and what you learn simply by being abroad.

Convinced yet? Read on.

2. Confronting "No"

"A ship in harbor is safe—but that is not what ships are built for." —John A Shedd

Don't expect everyone to be comfortable or happy with your interest in college abroad. In fact, you may get quite a bit of resistance from family and friends. It isn't usually because they're close-minded, or they're consciously trying to stop you; it is because they love you, want the best for you, and in their minds what is best for you is what they know. For this reason, negative reactions should be met with patience and sensitivity, as well as intelligent and insightful responses. This will go a long way in quelling people's doubts. This chapter covers the reactions that you may expect from people, how to respond, and more importantly, how to deal with that nagging voice in your own head telling you, "no."

The United States has the best education in the world

Americans tend to think that the United States has the best education in the world, and therefore, it isn't logical to go to college abroad. To be sure, we do have some of the best schools. According to the *Times Higher Education*, institutions in the United States make up 72 of the top 200 universities in the world, but this means, of course, that 128 of the top universities are located outside of the United States. Still, making a decision about where to go to college shouldn't be about going to the "best" universities, at home or abroad. The "best" universities, especially those in the United States, are usually the most exclusive and the most expensive. You may not have an opportunity at one of the top universities, even if you're a top student.

Most of us know there is more to consider than rankings. University rankings are politically driven and don't take into consideration the more nuanced and subjective things that make college an enriching experience. Employers want to see maturity, unique life experiences, and evidence of the ability to think and act independently and creatively. It is better to find the best "fit" for you, rather than the best university, which depends on what you want to achieve as a student and beyond. My master's program in Germany is certainly nowhere on the *Times Higher Education* top 200, but it was perfect for me.

Furthermore, it is somewhat elitist to assume that universities in your home country are always better than foreign universities. Students from around the world are doing quite well without an American degree. In fact, the United States has been slowly falling behind the rest of the world in education. The Programme for International Student Assessment (PISA) ranks Organization for Economic Co-operation (OECD) countries by the reading, math and science scores of 15 year-olds. In 2009, the United States ranked 14th in reading, 17th in science and 25th in math, out of 34 countries. Moreover, the United States currently ranks 13th in the world on educational competitiveness. Compared to other OECD countries, 25-34 year-olds in the United States are performing at what the World Economic Forum classifies as "subpar."

While these are regrettable statistics, I'm not suggesting that we simply give up and go somewhere else. What I am saying is that perhaps we shouldn't narrow our educational decisions to our own country. Due to different admissions philosophies, and a desire to admit more international students, it may be easier to get into the best university for a given subject abroad. According to yet another study conducted by the IIE in 2008, there is significant interest by schools in the regions of Europe, North America, and Oceania to increase their recruitment and enrollment of American students for full-time study.

You can't get a job in the United States with a foreign degree

Indeed, there may be some careers where a foreign degree would decidedly hurt your ability to get a job back in the United States, such as law. On the other hand, if your goal is to concentrate in an area of international law, or practice law in another country, having an international degree would be an asset. However, for many career paths there is no reason why a foreign degree should make it difficult or impossible to find a job in the US. There are plenty of non-Americans without American degrees that successfully find work in the US. What matters to most employers is that you have a degree, and above all that you can demonstrate your ability to problem-solve, think on your feet, work well with others, and be creative. Discussing your time living on your own abroad as a young student is a very concrete way to demonstrate that you have these skills. Imagine how your story will compare in a job interview to someone who earned a degree at the school down the street from where she grew up.

I've been there and here's what you should know

When I started advertising the fact that I was going to graduate school in Germany, several people who had been to or lived in Germany before took the opportunity to bestow upon me all their knowledge of my future home. As you can imagine, there were a wide range of impressions to sort through.

While it's tempting to get insider information, consider your sources carefully. Consider how long ago they were in the country, as well as the circumstances under which they stayed or lived. I talked to several people who had lived on American military bases in Germany. Some of what they told me turned out to be true, like the trains don't always run on time and not every German is proud of Oktoberfest. However, they also told me that apartments in Germany are empty shells, and you have to purchase *everything*, from the kitchen counters to the bathroom sink and install it yourself.

17

When I first heard these stories, I was flabbergasted, since I couldn't imagine designing an apartment on a student budget from the ground up. But after talking with current students on Facebook, I discovered that while many German apartments are in fact empty shells, there are plenty of other possibilities in terms of housing, especially for mobile students. German students commonly live together in what is called a *Wohngemeinschaft*, a room in a shared apartment that is usually furnished. I also learned that subletting furnished apartments is quite common. Naturally, those who lived on American military bases wouldn't have known about these housing solutions, since they had limited interaction with local Germans and students.

Don't take too seriously the advice from people who have merely passed through a particular city or country. Living in a country for an extended time is much different than visiting for a week or two. Most tourists have very little contact with locals and a superficial understanding of the culture; this is simply the nature of short-term travel. Sometimes locals are not friendly towards tourists, especially those who travel in large guided groups to popular attractions. Therefore, if a tourist comes away with the feeling that the local people were rude or off-putting, it may not be completely true. It may also be that what is considered rude by an American isn't considered rude in that country. I'm still a little taken aback by the, shall we say, lack of customer-oriented service in Berlin restaurants, but I've learned that this is not considered rude to Germans, and I can completely understand why the average American tourist would come away with this impression. It's simply a different idea of what constitutes good service; a nuanced clash of culture that a tourist is unlikely to understand. These kinds of sensitivities only develop after living in a country for a number of years.

No matter what people say, do your own research. Connect with current and former students by getting their email addresses from the university or connecting with the university's social networking sites. Search the blogosphere and get a travel guide as well. Ultimately, the country and its culture will speak directly to you. What *you* find charming may be different to someone else.

It is unsafe to move abroad

Between the media and the September 11th terrorist attacks, it's easy to get the impression that Americans are not well liked in the world, and that it's unsafe to live abroad. However, like all anxiety, it's important to put this in perspective. The United States homicide rate is among the highest in the world, and many foreigners find the number of guns in the US to be unnerving. American universities also have their fair share of violence and rape. Therefore, we shouldn't automatically assume that if we stay in the United States we will be safer. My family and friends were very concerned when I took a research fellowship in Jerusalem, a place of notoriously tense politics. I took these concerns seriously, and sought out advice from locals who told me that I should be okay as long as I was relatively smart and alert. Statistically speaking, there are very safe places to live beyond our borders (Sweden and Denmark come to mind). My point is simply that safety is less about location and more about behavior. How you comport yourself and how you exercise judgment will help to forgo problems both home and abroad.

I have never been met with hostility as an American living abroad. In fact, the vast majority of people I have met in such diverse places as Turkey, Morocco, Israel, Japan and Panama respect Americans. People often ask critical questions about American politics and foreign policy, and anyone who chooses to live abroad should be prepared for these types of questions. But never have I been questioned with malice or hatred; it has always been out of an intense desire to understand.

Those who choose to live abroad don't like the United States

It is no secret that in general Americans are extremely patriotic. However, patriotism doesn't reject other nations nor does it assume that to live in another nation is to reject your own. It is perfectly normal to take pride in where you come from and still find good in other countries. In fact, living abroad can actually deepen your sense of patriotism. By more thoroughly understanding your country from a multitude of angles, you'll likely appreciate things that are worth being proud of that you never would have considered without leaving the country. Of course, you may also discover things about your country that are undeserving of pride, and inevitably there will be times when you may feel ashamed or even angry. But to me this is true patriotism—knowing and understanding your country for all that it is, the good and the bad.

It's very expensive to do your college degree abroad

The higher education system in other countries can be very different than it is in the United States. One of the most striking differences is often the cost of attendance. Americans are often surprised to learn that going to college in many other countries doesn't cost tens of thousands of dollars. In fact, it can be tuition-free. Some countries and universities even grant small stipends to cover the cost of living.

Young people are facing an uncertain future in the United States, largely because of the high cost of education. In fact, student load debt recently surpassed credit card. Large debt makes life after graduation quite difficult. Even if you're lucky enough to find a well-paying job, writing a check every month for hundreds of dollars in student loan payments is a stifling obligation. Imagine what a difference it could make if you could get a degree without the debt. For example, you could take a job you're truly passionate about, even if it doesn't pay well. Avoiding debt and saving thousands of dollars is just one compelling reason to consider college abroad.

As you move down university rankings, the quality-to-cost ratio of a foreign degree improves significantly. For example, according to the Quacquarelli Symonds' (QS) ranking of the top 700 universities in the world, Seoul National University in South Korea ranks 42 and charges international undergraduates $6,000 per year in tuition while Carnegie Mellon in the United States ranks 43 and charges around $42,000. Similarly, the Swiss Federal Institute of Technology charges only $2,000 and is ranked 18, while the California Institute of Technology carries a $36,000 annual price tag for its rank of 12. In fact, if you chose to go to the *number two* university in the world—Cambridge—over the third best, Harvard, you'd get almost a 60% discount on your undergraduate education.

You'll miss the typical college experience

This statement assumes there is a "typical" college experience. However, universities in the United States go to great lengths to convince you that you'll have an extremely unique experience if you choose to attend their institution. Getting a "typical" experience, with the "typical" unemployment factor afterwards, is probably something that smart students are trying to avoid. It's much better to have an "atypical" experience that sets you apart from your peers, and makes you more competitive for jobs and graduate school.

On the other hand, there may be certain elements of the American college experience that are important to you, such as joining fraternities or sororities, or attending college football games. It is important to understand that you'll be doing very different things than your peers who stay in the United States, and if you really think you'll be "missing out," then going to college abroad probably isn't for you. However, if you're willing to sacrifice those things that typify an American college experience, you may in fact create a richer and more fulfilling experience in the end.

Going abroad is just an excuse to run away from your life

Some people may think you're running away from your life, but only you know if this is true. In any case, you should thoroughly consider whether you're ready to make a move overseas. If you are going through an emotional period, and you're using the opportunity to go abroad as a means of escape, consider postponing your journey. Of course, there is a big difference between running away from your problems and trying to improve and challenge yourself. It's true that changing one's environment helps to see things differently and brings some clarity to life. Although you may want to make your own decisions and take responsibility for the direction of your life, try to understand that some loved ones may take it as a rejection of them and the life they tried to give you. Don't be offended; point out that they may be part of the reason why you're so spirited and fearless, as to make such a life-changing move. If you've done your research and made the proper preparations, you'll show them that you're going for the right reasons.

You're too young to live on your own in another country

College abroad requires forethought, maturity, perseverance, and a certain amount of boldness. Being thousands of miles away has certain challenges that staying in the United States does not. If you feel lonely or overwhelmed, it may not be possible to fly home for the weekend to regroup. However, just because you're young, and you haven't lived on your own before or traveled abroad, doesn't mean you can't do college abroad. At some point in their lives, everyone has had to embrace their sense of adventure and throw themselves into the uncertain. You'll inevitably make mistakes and there will be moments of loneliness and sadness. Being ready isn't about having made all the preparations down to the last detail. No matter how much you plan, life will undoubtedly throw you a curveball. Being ready is just knowing you can handle the curveballs when they come. Many of us tend to underestimate ourselves, but when we challenge ourselves, we often rise to the occasion.

On the other hand, there is nothing wrong with accurately evaluating yourself, and where you are in your life, and deciding that you're just not ready for college abroad. It's not a one-shot opportunity. You can do your bachelor's or associate's degree in the United States and then consider getting a master's abroad. I hope that by reading this book you're able to get a general understanding of what it takes to do college abroad, and this will help you decide if it is something that you can handle at this point in your life.

3. College Abroad vs. Study Abroad

"I dislike feeling at home when I am abroad."
—George Bernard Shaw

You may be asking yourself why someone would enroll in a foreign university since most US universities, and private companies, offer study abroad programs. However, it is very important to understand that there are vast differences between college abroad and study abroad. Considering these differences will help you decide which is better for you. Keep in mind there are different types of study abroad programs that operate with radically different philosophies, and the picture I'm about to paint considers the *average* study abroad program.

Commitment

It may be an obvious point, but college abroad requires living abroad for a number of years. While the length of your degree program will vary by subject matter and country, the minimum amount of time is one year. Most study abroad programs, on the other hand, require living or traveling abroad for less than a year. Over 50% of US study abroad students participate in programs less than 8 weeks long, and 40% participate in programs for a semester or less.

Many study abroad programs are designed to make the experience as seamless as possible. Between your home and host institution, people will lead you through the process step-by-step. They'll give you a packing list, help you get a visa, and may even set up accommodations for you. If you're only going abroad briefly, minimizing time spent on administrative matters can help you maximize time spent studying and having fun. However, having everything taken care of for you really takes away from the experience of doing things on your own. If you enroll in a foreign university directly, the university will probably give you some help and guidance along the way, but you'll have to be much more self-reliant.

The first and perhaps most fundamental difference between college abroad and study abroad is finding your own accommodation. Your college abroad may offer you student housing, but it is important to know from the outset that many overseas universities do not offer housing that is comparable to US dormitories or amenities such as cafeterias and laundry rooms (unless it is a US-style residential institution). Therefore, it is important to weigh your options between off-campus and on-campus possibilities. Although finding private accommodation may be a difficult process, living off-campus has a number of advantages. You'll have your own room, as supposed to sharing a room with a total stranger. Living in an apartment may be nicer and more personal. Living on your own is more independent and you can come and go as you please.

The second thing you'll have to do is muddle through all the bureaucratic and administrative matters that are typical of moving abroad and starting a new university. While American undergraduate programs, including study abroad, are designed to at least temporarily replace the guidance and nurturance of a student's home life, with social activities and checklists of things to do and where to do them, you shouldn't expect the same step-by-step guidance from your college abroad. Many administrative matters will need to be worked through on your own, such as getting your student visa, registering with the local authorities, finding and registering for classes, getting local health insurance, opening a bank account, and arranging your finances. Some of these tasks may not even be required in a study abroad program. When you do these things on your own, you get to know the bureaucracy of the country as well as the university. It requires patience and maturity, but builds character and feels good when it's all over.

Experience

While I do not mean to belittle the study-abroad experience, eight weeks is not enough time to learn or become fluent in a language; it is not enough time to travel the country, and it is not enough time to integrate yourself into the local culture and shed your "foreigner" skin. If you choose to do a whole year abroad (which I would highly recommend!), you'll certainly get a deeper experience, but imagine how much richer the experience would be if it were two, three or four years.

Too often students treat their semester abroad as a vacation. It is hardly surprising that an 18 year-old traveling to Europe for the first time will take advantage of the nightlife. In fact, many US universities encourage students to take their study-abroad classes less seriously by granting only transfer or pass-fail credit. Many study abroad programs isolate foreign students by putting them all together in the same residence hall, placing them in the same set of classes, and setting up events designed exclusively for them. Although done with a customer–care approach, the result is that international students have too little time and too much structure to truly maximize the experience. Particularly for students with little prior experience with other cultures, or who are unsure of their language skills, it's too easy to spend the bulk of their time with other Americans.

Directly enrolling in a university abroad simply forces you to find yourself in your home away from home. You'll have plenty of time to party, and take classes for credit and integrate and see all the host country has to offer and learn the language with proficiency. You'll have the time to break out of your comfort zone, make true and lasting connections with people in your host country, as well as other international students, and learn the city as if you were a local. It was a deeply satisfying moment when I was able to go to the health insurance office in Berlin, and successfully negotiate for the cheapest plan in German. I'm sure I would not have been able to do this had I been a study abroad student.

Culture Shock

The type of "shock" you experience as a study abroad student is different from what you'll experience as a college abroad degree-seeking student. Study abroad programs are designed to mitigate the effects of culture shock. Why? Because positive student experiences make programs prosper, while negative student experiences kill them. In fact, I'm not convinced that study abroad students really experience culture shock at all precisely because many programs try to avoid it. In the first few months of living abroad they may experience some mild forms of homesickness, bewilderment, and disconnect. However, there is nothing "shocking" about these feelings, which are normal for anyone leaving their comfort zone, whether moving abroad or not.

Going to college abroad, you will experience something quite different. It will be much more intense; sometimes it will be profoundly lonely, and other times profoundly rewarding. You cannot fully prepare for the type of culture shock you'll experience, but it's the only way through which you can truly learn to appreciate a foreign culture.

Total Cost

It is extremely difficult to pre-determine the total cost of a study abroad experience, but if you include the tuition of a US university, plus program fees, it adds up. Some universities even charge higher tuition during the semesters you study abroad, and use part of it to compensate the host institution. This seems unfair if the host university charges local students a fraction of the tuition you're paying as a study-abroad student.

Even though the cost of living in a foreign country may be cheaper than the United States, it is hugely inflated by study abroad programs that create a familiar and comfortable environment for students. While many parents would be reluctant at the idea of spending tens of thousands of dollars on a European vacation, they don't seem to mind paying for a high-end study abroad program. If you're only interested in traveling, take a year off, buy a guidebook and get going. You'll see more on your own than you will on a study abroad program, and you'll save a ton of money.

If you choose to go to college abroad, you'll be getting a full-immersion experience for thousands of dollars less than staying in the US and doing a semester abroad. The United States charges by far the highest tuition in the world. Even in other countries that charge high tuition, it is much less than what you'd probably pay in the United States, even with financial aid and in-state tuition.

It is true that some overseas institutions charge higher tuition fees for international students, but again, it is usually much lower than the average in the US. It is worth noting that many American universities charge international students higher tuition fees as well. Still, many overseas institutions don't differentiate between local students and internationals and some don't charge tuition at all. I was taken aback when the local government in Bremen, Germany decided to increase their tuition fees for the public universities from nothing to around $800 per semester. Students and professors took to the streets to protest the action. To me, this was an extreme response, but from the German perspective, education is a right, not a privilege, and therefore the idea of charging tuition was seen as a violation of their rights

If going to college abroad means living in a country with a lower cost of living than wherever you would be living in the United States, then you could also save money. It depends on your personal living and spending habits. This may not be true for every country or city—London and Paris are of course two of the most expensive cities in the world (and VERY popular study abroad destinations I might add). However, as a fully enrolled student you can live modestly in a lesser-known city, with great local universities, and still be close to popular tourist destinations.

Competitiveness

Many students believe that going abroad will help pad their resumes, but it largely depends on you and the experience you have. Savvy employers can tell if your study abroad experience was truly a character-building exercise or just a prolonged vacation. As globalization deepens, employers will appreciate employees that are able to interface with offshore departments, work well with international partners, and negotiate the delicate dance of cross-cultural communication.

If you are thinking about studying abroad for career aspirations, ask yourself whether college abroad might actually be a better way to go. Make sure your degree will be recognized in the United States and the education you're receiving will be the type of training in your field that US employers value (that is, if you want to work in the US at all). In some cases, you'll need to get extra certifications back in the United States before you can work in the field.

4. Personal Considerations

"Do not follow where the path may lead. Go instead
where there is no path and leave a trail."
—Ralph Waldo Emerson

Going to college abroad is a very personal decision. It's important to utilize your resources and make an assessment of countries and universities that fit your personal situation. If you're moving with a family or your comfort zone isn't all that big, consider going to Canada, Australia, or the UK. If you're a woman, you may want to eliminate countries where women are known to occupy a lower-class status. The same is true if you're gay, lesbian, transgender or bisexual. Disabled individuals may want to limit their options to countries where they know they will have the facilities and support they need to thrive. Remember, you can always change your mind; even if you start college abroad and it turns out that you don't like it, you have the option to go home and transfer to a US university.

Language Abilities

If you're already fluent in another language, this opens up the world of college abroad almost immediately to wherever your language abilities apply. However, if your foreign language skills are rusty or non-existent, you can still do college abroad. You'll just need to make your choice of program carefully.

English is widely spoken throughout the world, especially in academia. Therefore, you may be surprised to find a plethora of English-language degree programs, even in countries where English is not an official language. This is truer of graduate programs than of undergraduate programs, but as you'll see in a later chapter, there are some English-language international bachelor's degrees available as well. In such programs, you'll have an obvious advantage as a native speaker.

Female Concerns

According to the Institute of International Education, women studying abroad have consistently outnumbered men by about two to one in the last ten years. Given this fact, there is no reason to believe that women can't be successful as college abroad students. However, any woman traveling alone should think carefully about location and take the appropriate precautions. The National Institute of Justice estimates that between one-fifth and one-fourth of women who attend college in the US become victims of sexual assault. So, don't assume that college abroad is automatically more dangerous than staying in the US. As a woman, you are more vulnerable to crime anywhere in the world. But you can minimize risk.

Use the State Department's website to assess security (travel.state.gov). Reach out to the university's international student office and other currently enrolled female students. Contact a local US university and ask about the incidents that have occurred on their study abroad programs in the country or city in question. Being the object of unwanted attention is the most common complaint of US women overseas. It's annoying, but rarely does it escalate into something more. Since you'll be spending considerable time abroad, you'll learn how to act like a local rather than being targeted as a tourist, and this reduces your risk. For more resources specifically tailored for women traveling or living abroad, see the website www.journeywoman.com.

Family Responsibility

Having a family complicates matters, but it should not make moving abroad impossible. Keep in mind that families all over the world are moving to new countries on a regular basis, either out of luxury or necessity. I've had the privilege of getting to know numerous professors in Europe who moved their families across borders as they moved from one university to the next. What struck me was their children's maturity, experiences, and foreign language abilities at such a young age. Although your children may not become hyper-polyglots or multicultural chameleons, think of the advantages they would have by becoming bilingual, speaking English at home and a second language at school. All the advantages that living abroad offers you will also apply to your family. Some countries actively support students with families by offering increased living stipends and on-campus childcare.

Unfortunately, if you're in a relationship but not legally married, taking your partner with you abroad may be difficult. Your partner won't be able to get a visa to stay in the country through any particular attachment to you. S/he would have to find a job or also enroll in a college abroad. Do your research ahead of time. Some cultures do not accept same-sex relationships at all, and therefore bringing your partner with you may put you at risk for significant discrimination and even crime. In some cultures you may even face difficulties in finding a landlord that will rent to an unmarried heterosexual couple. Other cultures may be more open-minded than the US about same-sex or unmarried couples, in which case you won't face discrimination and in fact you may live more comfortably than you would in the US. However, you'll still have to worry about what your partner will do abroad and how s/he will remain legal.

Check with the university regarding their policy on students with families. In many parts of Europe, it is quite common for university students to have families, both because there isn't a strong stigma against unmarried pregnant women and because students on average tend to be somewhat older than US students. However, having a family means you'll need a lot more money to go abroad than you would if you were going by yourself. Going to school full-time, or even part-time, makes earning money to support your family relatively difficult (and usually you can't get a student visa without studying full-time). As a student, your visa or residence permit may come with a limitation on how many hours per week you can work.

Furthermore, getting a job in a foreign country is not easy, especially if you don't speak the local language. If you're bringing your spouse, do some research before making any commitments regarding what types of jobs s/he may be able to do in the country. The best resources for this type of information are probably expatriate groups, many of which have websites for consultation. You can also join expatriate groups on social networking sites like LinkedIn, where you might also find job offers specifically for Americans living in those countries.

Ethnicity and Race

Your racial background may affect where you choose to go, depending on the experience you would like to have. While some countries are racially diverse, others are homogenous. Don't equate racial diversity with racial tolerance. A community may be diverse, but still guarded towards outsiders. Likewise, a homogenous community may readily accept someone from a different race. College abroad forces even Caucasian students to confront their racial identity, because they may be part of the minority in another country. If you're not a minority student in the US, being so abroad will certainly make the experience richer and deeper but also more challenging. Knowing what it feels like to be underrepresented is one of the best ways to become more tolerant and open-minded, and it can give you an incredible advantage in learning how to communicate with a diverse group of people.

Heritage may also be a motivating factor for choosing college abroad. Learning about your roots in their historical context can be a powerful and emotional experience. Although you may not be recognized as an outsider, don't think that going to the place of your heritage will decrease culture shock. In fact, it may increase culture shock due to unrealistic expectations. Furthermore, you may be accepted for your ethnicity but rejected, or not fully embraced, due to your nationality. It is important to understand that most countries have changed significantly from the time your grandparents or great grandparents lived there. Be prepared.

Spend some time researching stereotypes in your host country, specifically of your race. If stereotypes are negative, don't be discouraged. Carefully consider the extent to which you'll struggle and whether you're ready to accept those challenges. There's a difference between racist remarks and simple curiosity, even if somewhat ignorant. It is possible that people will misidentify your background, but again it may be due to innocent misunderstandings rather than malicious intentions. The exact intricacies of race relations in another country are best understood by spending a substantial amount of time abroad. Don't rely merely on stories from the news or your own stereotypes.

Disability

While there are countries that make having a disability challenging, due to lack of support and accessibility, you may be surprised to learn that there is a large international support network for international students with disabilities. In fact, some countries may be more supportive than the average US university. When you begin the application process, be sure to ask them what if any services are available for your disability. Even if they don't have a department or support group on campus, perhaps they can make arrangements specifically for you (like moving the rooms of the classes you take). Ask about accommodation either on or off campus that can meet your needs.

Before you leave, include on your medical bio sheet (to be discussed later) a detailed description of your disability. Learn the words in the local language that describe your condition, and any medication or other treatments that you require. Ask the university or current students about the extent to which the public transport system is accessible. Be prepared for an absence of things that you take for granted at home, such as accessible bathroom stalls and curb cuts. If you require a service dog, check with your host country's embassy ahead of time regarding the country-specific laws governing service animals. (See the International Association of Assistance Dog Partners, www.iaadp.org). People with disabilities may be treated differently in another country, but "different" isn't necessarily negative. Perhaps your best resource is Mobility International (www.miusa.org).

LGBT

Homosexuality is widely accepted in certain parts of the world, but other parts are at best skeptical and at worst, homophobic. Although anyone considering college abroad must do some personal reflection, members of the LGBT community will have to do a thorough interrogation of themselves and how their identity may interact with the local culture. How will you balance your sense of personal identity with conflicting norms in your host country? To what extent are you willing to bend your values for the experience of living abroad?

Know the legal status of homosexuality in your host country before you decide to go. Just being gay is considered a crime in some places. Even if homosexuality is legal, you may not be treated with kindness by authorities and others. A good resource for this information is the International Gay and Lesbian Human Rights Commission (www.iglhrc.org). There are also region- and country-specific websites and books that deal with LGBT issues and advocacy.

Understand what is considered sexually appropriate behavior both publicly and privately, how sexual and gender identities are understood, and what the coming-out process looks like. Familiarize yourself with the cultural codes surrounding dating and interactions between men and women. Consider compiling a list of gay-friendly organizations, support groups and businesses in your host city (see the International Lesbian and Gay Association and Global Gayz). If you plan to hide your sexual identity while abroad, you'll be living a double life of sorts when communicating with friends and family back home. This is also true if you plan to come out abroad, but you continue to hide your sexual identity back home.

In this vein, you should consider how going abroad will affect your entire life after you return. Will the same support system you had prior to leaving be available to you upon your return? Remember that you'll be abroad for a number of years and during this time, friends and family will change perhaps dramatically. Your relationships will have to adjust. It is not uncommon for people to dismiss any changes you've undergone, including coming out, as just a "phase." (The same may be said of changes *anyone* goes through while living abroad). Do your research and think things through. A great place to start is the Rainbow Special Interest Group of NAFSA or Frommer's Gay and Lesbian Europe.

Diet

If you regulate what you eat regardless of the reason, you'll have to pay more attention to where you go. For example, if you don't eat fish, it may be quite difficult to spend several years in Japan. On the other hand, if you're a vegan or vegetarian you'd probably do well in India (but some items may not be available or very expensive such as soy milk or vegan cheese substitutes). See www.vegdining.com and/or www.happycow.net; both websites have worldwide listings of vegan and vegetarian restaurants and supermarkets. Do your research ahead of time and get to know the local cuisine. You may have to cook for yourself more often and plan ahead when meeting friends for dinner.

Religion

Similar to race and heritage, your religion may be a reason to consider college abroad and where to go. Consider the following questions: How large is your religious community in the host country? What is the degree of religious tolerance? What is the relationship between religion and the government? Will you be free to wear religious symbolism? How does the culture perceive agnosticism and atheism? If you plan on being very open about your religious beliefs (or lack thereof) be prepared to encounter questions and criticisms, and know how to distinguish between inquisitiveness and aggression.

5. Affording College Abroad

"When preparing to travel, lay out all your clothes and all your money. Then take half the clothes and twice the money." —Unknown

While college abroad can be infinitely cheaper than college in the US, there *are* expenses. This chapter will help you plan for these expenses as well as for the unexpected.

Tuition

First consider tuition, if any. You might ask the university or current students whether tuition is expected to increase in the next few years. Be sure to make the appropriate calculations with the exchange rate. Although you can never be sure when it comes to the global market, you can look at the history of the exchange rate, which will either work in your favor or work against you. I've experienced both sides. When I was working on my master's degree, and transferring money from the US to Europe, it was disheartening to watch my $10,000 shrink to €7,000. Now that I'm receiving a stipend in Euros and transferring a little here and there to the US, it is nice to send €350 to my US account and see $450 appear.

International Airfare

You will need to budget the cost of flying to your destination country, and the cost of flying home once or twice a year. Use a high average figure. I'll discuss strategies for purchasing cheaper airfare later in this book.

Living Costs

If you want to save money on college abroad, avoid cities with notoriously high living costs, like Paris and London. But don't assume that all major "Western" cities are expensive. While the standard of living in Berlin is comparable to Paris and London, Berlin is much cheaper. Cost of living indices are accessible online for most major cities throughout the world. Universities may also provide basic expense guidelines on their website. These guides are usually created using the maximum you should expect to pay, so keep this in mind. To get a better sense of actual cost, try to get in contact with current students and ask them how much they spend on rent, food, etc. Ask them about options that students have to find low-cost accommodation, including both private and university housing. Ask if they know of anyone that is looking for a roommate, or if there is a website where students advertise rooms. Ask where the student-friendly neighborhoods are located.

Rent isn't the only thing that goes into a cost of living calculation. If you're getting a private apartment, you may also have to pay a range of bills including water, heat, electricity, television, Internet, trash pickup, and a building maintenance fee. Ask current students about their monthly bills as well. How these bills are calculated, and how often you have to pay them, will depend upon the specific location.

Food is also a huge expense. The university may offer a meal plan in which case you'll have to determine if it is worth your time and money. Meal plans are usually much more expensive than eating at home. If you're on campus frequently, the extra expense of a university meal plan might be worth the convenience. This is the most difficult expense to calculate, because you can hardly predict how your eating habits might change. Just plan on spending more than you anticipate.

Local Transportation

Transportation may be your next biggest expense, depending on where you'll be living. You will not likely have a car abroad, and monthly access to a city's public transport system can be either extremely reasonable or outrageous. When I was living in Hungary, I paid around $20 per month for unlimited access to the subways and buses. This is an absolute steal no matter how you look at it. In contrast, monthly access to public transport in Berlin is around $100 per month. However, with my special student transport card I paid around $240 *a semester* to use the public transport network. Don't forget that as a student with a valid ID you will probably be eligible for all sorts of discounts. There may be other ways to get around that save money, too, such as biking. Current or former students can tell you how most students get around and what they usually pay.

Health Insurance

You may have heard a lot about health care systems in other countries. If so, I implore you to ignore everything that you've ever heard, and get the information straight from the source. The fact of the matter is that generally speaking, health care is much cheaper in many countries than it is in the US, with comparable or higher quality of care, according to a detailed analysis conducted by the World Health Organization. Unlike study abroad programs, where your insurance will probably be included in the myriad of fees, you'll probably be required to have local health insurance as a college abroad student in order to get a visa.

The cost of health coverage will vary wildly depending on where you plan to go. Do your research beforehand. Some countries, like the UK, extend their national health service to non-citizens living in the country legally. This means that you'll have health coverage from the national system for free or for a small enrollment fee. Other countries may require non-citizens to purchase relatively expensive plans in order to be issued a residence permit. Your student status may also allow you to remain under your parents plan. Be careful about this option, however. Call the insurance company ahead of time to make sure your parents' plan will cover you overseas. Also, make sure that your host country will accept the coverage offered by your parents' plan for the purposes of getting a visa. When researching health insurance costs, be sure to inquire about student rates. Also, ask about average out-of-pocket expenses, deductibles, and the basic services that are covered.

Entertainment

Don't forget your "fun" money. Going abroad isn't all about studying hard and navigating bureaucracies. It's about really experiencing the country. You'll certainly want to budget for travel, and other leisure activities such as getting a few drinks on a Friday night, catching the latest movie, museum admission and so on. This is incredibly difficult to calculate ahead of time, but you can make a guess or set a budget and stick to it once you're there.

Scholarships and Stipends

Since numerous universities are trying to attract international students, they may offer scholarships to help defray the cost of tuition or living expenses. In some countries, there may be a central institution that administers scholarships, or maintains an up-to-date database for international students. Examples include the DAAD (www.daad.de) for Germany and Australian Education International (aei.gov.au). If you have a specific country in mind, look for organizations that facilitate exchange between the US and your target country; the Norway-American Association offers scholarships to American students planning to do their degree in Norway, as does the American Scandinavian Foundation. However, the trade-off of having a higher education system with little or no tuition is that there will probably be limited scholarship opportunities available in that country. Therefore, you might have to look beyond the university and the host country for additional sources of funding.

Institutions and groups in the United States may also offer scholarships. While undergraduate scholarships are rare, two of the most well-known and competitive graduate-school scholarships are the Marshall and the Rhodes Scholarships.

They offer full-ride funding that covers tuition and all living expenses for US students working on a graduate degree in the UK (only at Oxford for the Rhodes Scholarship). The coveted Fulbright Fellowship, sponsored by the State Department, also provides full scholarships to US students pursuing a graduate degree in another country. The Anne Wexler Foundation sponsors scholarships that allow US students to study public policy (at the master's level) in Australia. The Samuel H. Kress Foundation supports students going abroad to write their doctoral dissertation on European Art. There are innumerable fellowship opportunities for PhD students, which allow a student to be a visiting scholar at an overseas institution, usually for at least a year or more. Most PhD programs throughout the world come with some sort of funding, whether it is in the form of a stipend, a fellowship, or a work-study arrangement.

When I was looking for funding opportunities, I quickly discovered that there isn't much US funding available students going to college abroad, beyond the prestigious and highly competitive programs I mentioned above. I suspect this may change sooner or later, as college abroad becomes a more attractive and popular option among students in the United States. A recent article, "Outsource your Kid" (January 30, 2012) in *Foreign Policy Magazine* makes the case that US students would benefit from enrolling in overseas institutions, and calls for prestigious government-sponsored programs like Fulbright grants to be open to undergraduates, and the Gilman Scholarship to consider full-degree applicants.

Loans

It's possible to get a degree abroad without debt, especially if you find a program that charges little or no tuition. However, loans may be a source of funding for college abroad if you need some extra help. Your debt could be less than it would be if you went to college in the US, if you are fortunate enough to have lower tuition, lower cost of living, and/or a shorter degree program.

Federal loans are usually the first source that US students tap to finance their college education. They generally

41

have favorable interest rates and flexible repayment plans. The catch is that in order to receive a federal loan, the school must be approved by the Department of Education. There are quite a few overseas institutions that are eligible, but most of them are in Western Europe and Oceania. You can check to see if your school qualifies by going to the website of the Free Application for Federal Student Aid (FAFSA). Use the Federal School Code Search Tool and select "Foreign Country" under State and then type in the city.

Another source for education loans are private lending agencies. Use this as a last resort, because loans from private lenders are usually not as flexible as federal loans, and come with higher fees and interest rates. However, if you only need a small amount of money to help cover living expenses, a private loan might be your best option. First, approach your local bank that you've been a customer of for a number of years. As a loyal customer, they may offer you good interest rates and repayment terms. Unless you already have a top credit rating, you might need a co-signer on the loan.

Some colleges abroad may offer the possibility for students, even international students, to apply for loans in the host country. As more private universities have surfaced in Germany, for example, schools have made arrangements with Deutsche Bank to give loans to international students. This arrangement, however, is not common and is usually difficult for a foreigner due to a lack of credit history in the country.

Work Abroad

Check with the embassy of the host country as to whether or not you'll be allowed to work with your visa. You'll either have a student visa or a residence permit, and each comes with potentially strict labor regulations. If you're allowed to work, see if your university offers jobs for students. These are the types of jobs that a student can most easily attain and can be scheduled around class. However, student jobs don't pay well, and it is unlikely you'll be able to afford your entire cost of living through part-time employment. You may be able to get an off-campus job, but 20 hours is usually all you are permitted to work per week. If you don't speak the local language well, getting an off-campus job may be challenging. Don't forget that if you do work, you'll have to pay taxes, and in some countries taxes are much higher than in the US. Not only that, but if you make over a certain limit, you may be liable for taxes both locally *and* to the United States government. (See Publications 54, 593 and 901 from the IRS, www.irs.gov).

Some students supplement their income by being particularly resourceful and creative. One American student in Germany used the breaks between semesters to work as an au pair for German families. While getting paid and living rent-free with German host families, she was also able to become fluent in German. This may be an ideal way to spend vacation between semesters, as flying home could be expensive. Other students I know offered their English language skills for a modest fee to people in the local community. You might have another talent that you can "market" to make a few extra euros, rupees, or pounds. If you sing or play piano, for example, you can offer lessons below market value to students or members of the community. I've known students to sell art both locally and online, and I even know a student with a massage therapy certification who opened a massage studio. Working overseas will probably only supplement your living costs; it won't likely cover your entire stay. Think of working abroad as a way to make some pocket money for those nights when you want to unwind with a local beer and your host country's equivalent of pizza.

Personal Savings

If you're going to an overseas institution, particularly one that doesn't charge tuition, you may be able to live from your personal savings. While it may be tempting to take your summers off, consider working and saving instead. With proper planning and sacrifice, you may be able to save enough money in the six to nine months prior to your departure. If you plan to attend a three-year bachelor's program, or an intense bachelor's program that translates into a bachelor's-master's degree in the US (like in the United Kingdom and Australia for example), then taking a year off to work and save may actually be a good financial decision.

Simplify Life

If you want to have more money to spend while you're living abroad, there are a number of things you can do to simplify your life in the US and free up some cash. First, go through all of your possessions to identify things that can be donated or sold. Selling some of your old stuff will probably not yield a ton of extra money, but every little bit helps. Items that are donated may also be a tax write-off, if you itemize rather than use the standard deduction. Hold a garage sale or advertise your stuff online through Craigslist, eBay, or Amazon. Sell heavy appliances like coffee makers or even your hairdryer. You can't take these things with you because they won't work with your new country's electricity outlets and voltage. If you have old textbooks from a previous degree that you know you'll never use again, take them to a university bookstore or sell them on Amazon.

If possible, pay off any outstanding balances on your credit cards before leaving or consider transferring your balance to another card with a 0% APR for 12 months or longer. If you have several credit cards that you don't use often, cancel them. I recommend going abroad with only one or two credit cards in your wallet. Switch to cards that don't charge a foreign transaction fee, have no annual fees, and are associated with a travel rewards or a cash-back program. If you're not going to be drawing from your savings, move what you can to a high-yield savings account such as a CD. Investigate whether you as a foreigner can open a high yield account in your destination country, and compare the rates (taking into consideration the exchange rate). If the exchange rate works in your favor, and you open an account with a higher interest rate in your host country, then you'll make more money by moving a substantial portion of your savings abroad with you (this depends also on the local cost of living).

Next, cancel all monthly subscriptions or memberships you might have in the US, well in advance of leaving. Cancel your cable contract early and opt for Hulu or iTunes instead. Cancel your landline as well and use Skype or your cell phone. Some of these vendors will probably try to make it difficult for you to get out of your contract, but in my experience, persistence pays. You may have to produce proof that you're actually

44

moving abroad. Cell phone providers don't advertise it, but many of them will allow you out of the contract, without paying the cancellation fee, if you can show that you're really moving abroad. I called my provider (T-Mobile) before I left the country and explained to them the situation. Once I arrived in Germany, I faxed them a copy of my rental agreement and student ID and they let me out of my contract and waived the cancellation fee.

If you're paying rent in the US, either get out of your lease or sublet your apartment. This requires entrusting your apartment to someone you know well and having him or her manage the sublet while you're gone. If possible, move in with your parents for a few months before you leave, to save rent money, or get a roommate, to split the rent. Arrange with your landlord beforehand to get back as much of your security deposit back as possible. If you own a home, you may also consider renting it out while you're away. This is a great way to have extra monthly income, but doing so requires you to work with someone back home to make the arrangements. Depending upon the housing market, it may make more sense to sell your property and use the cash from the sale to finance your stay abroad. For better information about managing your housing situation while abroad, visit http://meetplango.com. They help people take career breaks and sabbaticals to live abroad for a substantial amount of time.

Similarly, if you have a car, consider selling it. The money from the car will be very useful to you while you're abroad, and it will only depreciate if you let it sit at home in the US. Go through your bank account or credit card statement at the end of any given month and look at what expenses can be reduced or eliminated. I broke my Starbucks habit before moving abroad and opted instead to drink the free filtered coffee available in my office. Five dollars may not seem like a lot, but if you abstain from your daily latte, that is $25 per week, $100 per month. If you give up expensive coffee for just six months prior to your trip, you'll have an extra $600 in your pocket—enough perhaps for the international airfare. By far my biggest expense was going out to eat, so I forced myself to cook more at home. Honing your cooking skills will also be a money-saving strategy that you can use overseas.

If you have a monthly student loan payment from a previous degree, it may be possible to defer your payments on federal student loans. A deferral simply means that payments are temporarily suspended under certain circumstances. There are several reasons that a student loan can be deferred, and reentering school is one of them. Unfortunately, the school must be one that is officially recognized by the US Department of Education to qualify. Doctoral students who are receiving a "fellowship" can also apply for deferral (and it doesn't matter if the program is recognized by the Department of Education or not). Another option is to apply for a financial hardship deferral. For this, you have to prove that your income is less than a certain threshold. Obviously if you're going to school abroad you probably won't be working and your income will be zero. Work with your loan servicer to apply for deferment. Note, interest continues to accrue on the loan even in deferment, but every quarter you'll have the opportunity to pay off the total interest that accumulated over the previous period. If you choose not to defer your loans, you have other options. There are a few different repayment plans available for federal loans, and you can switch to the plan with the lowest monthly payment. If you haven't consolidated your loans yet, do so. Consolidation simplifies your repayment plan and often decreases the amount of interest you're paying. You can set up automatic payments online so you won't have to worry about paying the loan while you're away.

Transportation while Traveling

To date, I've traveled to over 30 countries, most of them while I was studying overseas, with no income whatsoever. Ironically, I didn't do any foreign travel while I was working and making a substantial salary in Chicago. Why? Because foreign travel is less dependent on money and more dependent on time. Having a full time job gives you money, but it doesn't give you a lot of time. If you can learn how to travel like a backpacker and less like a stereotypical American tourist, you can take advantage of the more flexible hours you have as a student and see even more of what the world has to offer.

Once you're "overseas," getting to other countries beyond your host country, or traveling within your host country, can be easy and cheap. Again, local students may be the best resource. Don't assume that flying is always the most expensive option. There are plenty of discount air carriers throughout the world, which provide regional services for sometimes unbelievably low fares. I was able to fly to Paris from Germany on a carrier called Ryanair for less than 20 euros. These flights are extremely bottom-dollar: quite literally all you get is an uncomfortable seat with even less legroom than your typical seat in economy class. However, beware! They add little fees here and there, such as a fee for using your credit card and a fee for checking in at the airport instead of online. They also have stringent baggage limitations with more fees if you go over. If you don't take these things into consideration, the cost of the flight can add up.

Trains are another option. Trains in many parts of the world are safe and reliable. However, the affordability of train travel varies widely by country, even within Europe. It cost me just a few dollars to travel between cities on the train in Morocco and Romania, but connections between cities in Germany can cost well over $100. If you can withstand some discomfort, night trains are a great way to save money while traveling. It saves you the cost of a hotel room, and a ticket on the night train is usually less expensive than a comparable ticket during the day. You can sit in a regular seat and try to sleep, or you can pay more and get a sleeper car. Trains often have group discounts—organize a weekend away with friends and pay the group rate. And don't forget about any student discounts.

Besides flights and trains, many countries are well connected through an extensive network of bus lines. Another option to consider is ride shares, in which people with a car who are driving to a certain destination offer a seat in their car for a small fee. Inquire with local students regarding the safety of this option, but generally, such an arrangement is safe and another good way to practice your language skills. Hitchhiking is a common practice in many countries, and although it has some risk, it is generally a relatively safe and completely free way to get around. If you pursue this option, it is best to do it with another person, especially if you're a female. Ask local students about the etiquette involved.

Accommodations

If you'll be living off-campus, live with roommates. It is also a great way to make local friends and practice your language skills. Look for a room in a shared student apartment that is already furnished so you don't have to buy furniture or other necessities like sheets and towels. If there are things that you need for your apartment that aren't provided, advertise your needs over the student network. Many universities have created something like a Craigslist for the student body, where students buy and sell things for student-friendly prices. Outgoing students are always looking to get rid of things.

Cooking at home is much less expensive than eating out. It's also generally healthier, unless you're eating frozen pizza every night. Growing up, I didn't cook much, but living abroad changed me and now I like experimenting with new recipes. The Internet is full of free recipes. Keep in mind that some of the ingredients you consider staples in the US may be unavailable or expensive in other countries, but you won't know until you arrive. Arrange a cooking schedule with your roommates so that you'll cook once or twice a week and they'll cook once or twice a week, thus saving you both time and money. You can do the same with others outside of your flat. For example, organize potluck dinners with other international students every month, in which each student brings a dish from his or her country.

Although watching local television is an excellent way to learn the language, think about the cost-detriment; some countries may have a few public channels you can watch free. Consider whether you'll need Internet at home as well. Sharing wireless Internet not only with your roommates but also with neighbors can save money. If you do get high-speed Internet access, it may be redundant to also have a television and a landline phone. Some countries make their public television available online legally for free. For a few bucks, you can also get legal access to US television and movies through online services such as iTunes.

I never stay in hotels when I travel. I've stayed in hostels that quite literally resemble a palace in Morocco, a modern art gallery in Copenhagen, and an antique store in Reykjavik. I really can't imagine paying $100 or more a night for a stiff cookie-cutter hotel. What makes hostels affordable is the fact that in general, you stay in a dorm room with other travelers. And like a dormitory, bathrooms, including showers, are also shared. I know this offends the American sense of privacy, but remember that many dormitories on US university campuses operate on the same principle. For a few extra dollars a night, many hostels offer private rooms with private bathrooms as well. Safety has never been a concern for me at a hostel. Websites like Hostel World (www.hostelworld.com) allow users to rate the hostels on criteria such as safety, character, affordability, and cleanliness.

Another option is couch surfing. Much like ride shares, people with an extra room, bed or couch in a particular city advertise on www.couchsurfing.org and travelers passing through can contact them and arrange a free stay. Safety is created through the community network and reviews from both travelers and home stays, and of course, good old-fashioned common sense. Staying with a local who can provide insider information about the city is quite a luxury, all for practically nothing. Once you get to know local students, you'll probably find yourself with invitations to go home with friends or join them on a weekend getaway. Take advantage of these invites! This is a great way to see another part of the country and see how the average person lives.

Avoid Tourist Traps

You've finally made it to your dream destination of Venice and you're eagerly looking to hire a gondola for what you hope to be a tour of a lifetime. But your jaw may drop when you discover the voyage will cost you €80 for 40 minutes. Tourist traps are called so for a reason—they will trap your money. If it is really something you've been dreaming about, and you're fairly certain you may not return, the $100 might be a splurge you can justify. However, you may decide that such an expense isn't worth it, since you can see the city of Venice just as well by meandering through the streets and over the bridges, or taking a ride on the bus ferries.

The most important things to see and do in a city don't usually cost a ton of money. You can take hundreds of photos of the Eiffel Tower for free, but it will cost you €14 to go to the top. What I enjoy most is simply sauntering through the streets, stopping at cafes for a cheap bite, observing how the people dress and how they communicate, and trying to really feel the rhythm of the city. These are likely to be lasting impressions of a place when you travel, and they are mostly available to you for free.

International Student ID

Get an International Student ID card (ISIC) before you leave. You might read some travel blogs that say this card isn't worth it, and in fact that might be true if you're only traveling internationally for a few weeks. But if you're living abroad and traveling often, and sometimes spontaneously, the card will probably save you more than the $22 it costs per year. Even if a student discount isn't displayed at museums and other sights, just ask. You can also use this card for discounts when and if you go home for a visit in the US. The card can be purchased in most locations overseas as well.

6. Finding a College Abroad

"A journey of a thousand miles must begin with a single step." —Lao Tzu

Finding a college abroad can be a daunting task. Fortunately, most schools, especially those wishing to draw attention from international students, have a website. There are also website directories for colleges abroad, where you can search by country, subject, and other terms. Considering the vast number of institutions across the globe, you'll need an understanding of the different types of institutions and a strategy for narrowing your search.

Branch Campuses

If you're committed to having an overseas experience but still feel you want a US degree and close ties to a US school, there are a number of American universities that have branch campuses abroad. Some of these programs allow a student to directly apply to the overseas branch and complete the degree entirely abroad, while others require an application through the university in the United States. Some of these arrangements are true "branch" campuses in which the student lives on the international campus and is awarded a degree from the American university. Other models are less direct, where American universities coordinate activities and exchanges but the degree is not awarded by the American university. Either way, students abroad get the benefit of the investment and name recognition of the US school.

It is important to note that the number of "branch" campuses overseas has been steadily declining since the financial crisis of 2008. Michigan State, George Mason, and Suffolk University recently closed their overseas branches in Africa and the Middle East. US schools have discovered that maintaining overseas branches can be costly. Complicating matters are the objections of some who contend that US institutions should not be opening campuses in places with questionable human rights records.

Nonetheless, there are still quite a few American universities operating some type of international "branch." New York University has been rather successful in this endeavor, having maintained an Abu Dhabi campus since 2005. A unique arrangement known as Education City has cropped up in Qatar, where six American universities (along with a local institution, a French and a British school) support international branches of their respective campuses. Yale is opening its doors to a cooperation with a campus in Singapore. Carnegie-Mellon is offering a master's program in Information Technology in Rwanda.

Some smaller, lesser-known and mostly private institutions in the US have long maintained partnerships or branches abroad. McDaniel College has sustained its overseas campus in Budapest since 1995, where students can complete their degree in Hungary but also have the option to attend the American campus in Maryland. Alliant International University has locations throughout California as well as programs in Japan, China, Italy, and Mexico. Webster University's main campus is near St. Louis but has successfully maintained campuses for a number of years in the Netherlands, Austria, China, Switzerland, Thailand and the United Kingdom. Similarly, Schiller International University, with its base in Florida, also offers campuses in Spain, Germany, and France.

Although these opportunities have the advantage of taking part in a true American program entirely overseas, the majority of them charge tuition rates similar to what you would pay in the US. However, because many of the programs are

US-accredited, most are eligible for federal student loans and most offer scholarships, grants, and work-study programs. Students considering one of the new international branches should do so with caution, as these are still experimental.

International Dual and Joint Degree Programs

Joint degree programs represent a structure in which a student takes courses given by two or more schools leading to *one* degree certified by all institutions involved. Dual degree programs result in *two* degrees, one from each institution, on an accelerated schedule. Both allow students to attend more than one school and provide an extensive and in-depth experience with a foreign institution and an American university. These arrangements allow a student to put more than one university and potentially more than one area of specialization on his or her resume.

Unlike many study abroad programs, students in joint and dual degree programs are fully enrolled in their respective overseas institutions. Students must go through an application process in which all institutions are involved in the admission decision. This is different from a study abroad program, where the application process is done through the home university. Study abroad programs tend to focus more on the living experience, while joint and dual degree programs balance both the living and academics.

According to a report issued by the Institute of International Education, the majority of joint and dual degree programs offered through American universities are targeted towards undergraduate students, yet I was able to find several programs aimed towards master's and doctorate students as well. Tuition for these types of programs, especially if offered through an American university, will probably compare to what you'd pay to go to college in the United States and perhaps even more in order to compensate the foreign institution. Law and business degrees seem to be particularly popular. New York University offers dual law degrees with its satellite campus in Singapore as well as Melbourne Law School in Australia. Similarly, Cornell Law offers dual degree programs with partner institutions in France, Germany and China. Yale has a partnership with the Universidad de los Andes in Colombia in which students earn a dual degree in Business Administration and Forestry Management. The University of San Diego allows students to earn an MBA along with a master's in science in either Mexico or Germany. The International Master's in Management Program is a joint endeavor of Purdue, Technische Universiteit Eindhoven (The Netherlands), Central European University (Hungary), and the GISMA Business School Hannover (Germany).

Joint and dual degree programs are not limited to the United States, however. Europe has been doing this far longer than we have. The Global Studies Programme provides a joint master's and PhD with institutions in Germany, India, South Africa, Thailand and Argentina. My doctorate program (the Berlin Graduate School for Transnational Studies) is a joint initiative between the Freie Universität Berlin, the Social Science Center Berlin (*Wissenschaftzentrum Berlin*) and the Hertie School of Governance. For European master's programs, search the Master's Portal EU (www.mastersportal.eu).

The Erasmus Mundus program assists in the creation of joint degree programs within Europe and between European and non-European countries. It also provides a competitive scholarship scheme for students participating in eligible programs. A full list of current Erasmus Mundus master's and doctorate programs can be found on the website, and the majority of these graduate programs are offered in English, at least in part (http://eacea.ec.europa.eu/erasmus_mundus). The ALGANT program offers joint master's and doctorate degrees in algebra, geometry and number theory through institutions in France, Italy, the Netherlands, India, Canada and South Africa. The Common European Master's Course in Biomedical Engineering offers a double degree among universities in the Netherlands, Germany, Ireland, Belgium and the Czech Republic. The International Master of Science in Rural Development is a collaboration between universities in Belgium, France, Germany, Slovakia, Italy, the Netherlands, South Africa, Ecuador, India and China. Finally, the Doctorate Programme on Marine Ecosystem Health and Conservation has 23 total partnerships in countries ranging from Poland, Lithuania, and Norway to Australia and the United States. Most of these programs, especially those that offer the opportunity to study at non-European universities, charge tuition fees, which are reasonable compared to the United States. Because these programs are supported by the Erasmus Mundus program, full scholarships are also available.

American Universities and Models

Unlike overseas branches, some universities overseas have independently adopted the American model of higher education. These schools, although often containing "American" in the name, are often not affiliated with the American government. Universities in this category are likely to be residential, at least for some section of the student population, with a substantial on-campus support system, student clubs and organizations, as well as sports and arts facilities. Perhaps the most important and notable characteristic of these schools is the fact that the education will follow a liberal arts model, in which students have a wide variety of academic and extracurricular activities from which to choose. Undergraduate students don't have to choose a major course of study right away until they've "sampled" some introductory courses. Like many US undergraduate programs, students will probably be required to take a number of survey courses in a variety of fields, in addition to the specialized courses in his/her major. This is an important difference because some non-US institutions steer you towards your major immediately upon enrollment or during the application process, in which applicants apply to a specific program or school.

An American student attending this type of school will have the best of both worlds: a familiar education model in an unfamiliar country. Although an American school will offer some of the comforts of home, it will inevitably borrow from the local culture. The grading system, for example, will probably be according to local standards. Certain social norms will be upheld within the culture of the school, even if they do not conform to American tradition. Students living in the dormitories at the American University of Cairo are strictly segregated by gender, for example. For some, attending an American overseas institution may not be challenging enough culturally, but attending an American school overseas would be more challenging than attending a branch campus. However, when attending an American overseas university, it is possible that you inadvertently create a "bubble" for yourself in which interaction with the local culture is avoided, invalidating the most important aspect of college abroad.

A very quick way to find a college abroad that fits into this category would be to do an Internet search for "American University of." You'll discover there are dozens of American universities all over the world. Examples include the American University of the Caribbean, American University of Beirut, American University of Dubai, and the American University of Central Asia. Other examples include John Cabot University in Rome and the American College of Thessaloniki in Greece. More often than not, these universities are designed to attract top quality local students as well as a substantial pool of international students. The faculty is likely either American or American-educated. They are nearly all private, not-for-profit liberal arts institutions. Sometimes they are accredited not only by an authority in the country in which they are located but also by a US authority. On the downside however, American universities overseas oftentimes come with an American price tag. Yet, check out the American College of Greece, a school founded by Americans in 1875 with extremely low tuition fees. And even though they are "American" schools, they still may not be eligible for federal student loans.

Beyond the American universities, there are plenty of other examples of overseas institutions that operate on the American model of higher education. My alma mater, Jacobs University, borrows aspects of the American model as well as the British model, and was specifically designed to attract international students. Other examples include Antalya International University in Turkey, Vesalius College in Brussels, Belgium, the International University of Monaco, Roosevelt Academy in Middelburg, Netherlands, and Franklin College in Lugano, Switzerland.

Included in this category would also be schools that, due to cultural and historical similarities to the US, happen to offer similar collegiate experiences to what one would have in the US. By this I mean schools in countries such as Canada, the

UK, Ireland, Australia and New Zealand. Attending a university in any of these English-speaking countries would probably be the least difficult for an American student, given the language, common culture and similar higher education model. However, it is important to note that although there are many parallels between universities in the English-speaking world and American universities, there are notable differences. At most British institutions, one has to commit to a course of study during the application process even as an undergraduate. If you know what you want to study, this is good because you'll be able to start your major courses right away. It also allows you, in some cases, to finish your degree more quickly than you would in the US—a bachelor's degree in the UK takes three years instead of four. In fact, the University of Buckingham offers bachelor's degrees in just two years. In terms of cost, it is difficult to say whether attending an institution in an English-speaking country would save you money. Tuition rates are generally much higher for international students than for local students. Due to the cultural exchange, many of these schools are eligible for federal loans, although check with FAFSA to be sure.

Foreign Universities

The last type of college abroad is the local foreign university, with the education system of its own country. Just as there are a multitude of colleges and universities in the US with different missions, structures, and target student population, the same applies to all the other universities around the world. Don't be alarmed if residential dormitories are lacking and there are fewer extracurricular options. And don't assume that all the universities in that country are the same, since the types of universities that exist within any given country can vary greatly. You're likely to encounter public universities, research institutions, private universities and colleges, corporate for-profit institutions, gender segregated universities, religiously affiliated universities, international universities, and the list goes on.

There are a few more things to keep in mind. First, any school you consider (and this advice should also be applied to any school you consider in the United States) should at least be recognized by the country's Ministry of Education. Most non-US institutions are not US-accredited. This doesn't mean that your degree will be worthless in the US; it just means that a governmental agency has reviewed the institution and has approved it. Accreditation is an insurance policy that you're getting an education that meets some standards. There have also been a recent wave of *for-profit corporate* institutions surfacing both abroad and in the US that are essentially unrecognized and unaccredited "diploma mills" meant to scam you out of your money. *For-profit* universities are primarily run as business ventures with corporate shareholders, while private schools are usually classified as charitable or not-for-profit organizations. Don't confuse private universities with *for-profit,* and don't assume that public universities are inferior to private universities. Some of the best universities in the world are public, such as the Swiss Federal Institute of Technology in Zurich. Furthermore, many countries don't have a strong history of private education. The distinction between public and private is simply meant to distinguish between the amount of funding and other support the university receives from the government.

Protect yourself by verifying the school's proper recognition or accreditation. Be leery if the school charges higher than normal tuition or refuses to disclose its tuition fees until after you've enrolled. If the school promises an immeasurably profitable career upon graduation, or pressures you into getting a student loan (even if you think you can afford the cost of education without loans), you may want to stay clear. Finally, make sure the university has at least a small office dedicated to international students. The school should be open and willing to help international students. There are schools that, due to any number of reasons, simply aren't equipped to deal with international students. If you have a strong background in the culture and language, you may be able to thrive at a school without the means to support international students, but most students will want at least some minimal level of support.

Many bachelor's programs in Europe are three years. This means that those who enter a bachelor's program are really expected to operate at the sophomore level when they begin. Don't let this scare you. The freshmen year at most US universities is merely a transition period, and the coursework is often lighter than the last three years.

Area of Study

Perhaps the most important thing to consider is your area of study. If you're not sure what you want to study, consider American-style liberal arts institutions outside of the US. If you already know what you want to study, it's better (but not absolutely necessary) for you to choose a college with a dedicated course of study. Should you enroll in a dedicated course of study, make sure you understand how to change academic tracks, just in case you change your mind.

Be sure you understand what your intended degree and major means in the national context. While many countries have implemented or are in the process of implementing the Bologna Process, meaning they offer bachelor's, master's, and doctorate degrees along the same lines as the degrees awarded in the US, some countries offer different types of degrees. For example, you might also see degrees such as D.Phil or M.St. or M.Sc. If you decide to pursue a degree that is generally not offered by American schools, just make sure you understand the rough equivalent of the degree in the US system. A BA degree done at Oxford, for example, is considered a much more specialized degree than BA degrees in the United States. Finally, don't assume that if you pursue a type of degree that isn't usually offered in the US that your degree will be invalid in the US, especially if it is coming from a place as well known as Oxford or Cambridge. You may need to ask the university for a degree supplement containing a brief description of the degree and how it translates to a US degree.

Narrow your search for a college abroad by focusing on schools that are well known in your subject area. If you're interested in French literature, consider college abroad at one of the many fantastic universities in France, such as Science Po or Pierre & Marie Curie University. You can also ask for some recommendations from an advisor and your current teachers or professors. Perhaps you would like to work with a renowned scholar with similar interests. Don't narrow your search to the "obvious" choices. Although Greece may be famous for inventing the Classical Style, this isn't the only place to study architecture. China has a long history of ancient architecture, as well as stunning examples of modern architecture. Parts of the Middle East have gone through a massive architectural revolution in recent years, and have invested heavily in English-language higher education, too.

If you're undecided with an interest in two subjects, or if you have a specific career objective that requires knowledge in two areas of expertise (like business and environmental science for example), consider a dual degree program. Perhaps there is an organization abroad that you'd be interested in working for someday. Choosing a school in that country, or a university that has an internship or other affiliation with that organization would be a great way to kick start your career.

English-Language Programs

If you're uncomfortable with your foreign language skills, you may narrow your search to programs taught entirely in English. English is the international language of academia. Textbooks, prominent journals, and most of the largest research databases are in English. If original texts were not written in English, they have probably been translated. English language programs can be found throughout the world, even in places where English isn't normally spoken on the streets. In fact, English-language (or dual-language) programs are proliferating throughout the world in nearly every academic discipline.

It may be difficult to find an English undergraduate degree program in a non-English speaking country. A few English language programs have surfaced in the Middle East (e.g. University of Qatar) and Asia (e.g. University of Hong Kong and National University Singapore). The Hogeschool-Universiteit in Brussels offers a three-year bachelor's program in Business Administration. You may also find English degree programs in locations such as South Africa and India, or "international" universities. Check the Erasmus Mundus database, which is primarily dedicated to master's programs, but offers a few bachelor's programs, too.

If you plan to enroll in an English-language degree program, you should make an effort to learn at least some of the local language. Take advantage of being able to speak English at school while becoming fluent in the local language by making local friends and taking classes if time permits. Knowing some basic phrases and vocabulary will help you communicate with local students and facilitate the integration process. In any English-language program, you'll probably find yourself in an odd sub-culture that makes learning the local language strangely difficult. It's easy to gravitate towards other English-speakers, and conveniently avoid the local language. To circumvent this problem, establish an informal agreement from the moment you meet people that you will speak the local language instead of English. If non-native speakers want to practice their English, too, work out a half-and-half agreement.

You don't have to be fluent in order to enroll in courses that are taught in the local language. You need a certain level of skill, however, which you'll need to demonstrate during the admissions process. Think of some of the international students that come to the US each year to study—they have a good grasp of English but many are not completely fluent. Enrolling in a degree program in a foreign language is one of the fastest ways to become fluent in that language. The first semester or year may be a struggle, but if you completely immerse yourself, there's no reason why you can't be speaking and reading the language well in a matter of months. Some universities offer (or require) that international students come early to take language classes before the semester begins. Many cultural exchange organizations will even pay for these preparatory language classes, like DAAD, the German Academic Exchange Service.

Master's Programs

If you're pursuing a master's degree, you may see two different types of programs, especially in Europe or British-affiliated universities: "taught" and "research." Taught programs consist mainly of coursework (lectures, tutorials and seminars), culminating in a small paper or thesis at the end. Research programs, as the name suggests, are carried out primarily through an independent and lengthier project, with only light coursework. Before deciding, think about your preferred learning style, and which type of degree is best suited for your goals. You will probably apply directly to specific master's program, rather than through a university-wide system. If Europe is of interest to you, the Master's Portal EU database (www.mastersportal.eu) should be your first stop.

Doctorate-level Programs

There are also many doctorate-level *programs* throughout the world. By programs, I mean a structured arrangement in which the student engages in coursework as well as research and dissertation writing. With a structured PhD program, you will apply through a regular call for admissions the same way you would to a master's or bachelor's program. This is in sharp contrast to the more traditional way to earn your doctorate, in which you find a professor or group of researchers engaging in the specialty that interests you and approach them directly about a possible PhD position in their department. There may not be formal calls for these positions. Rather, you have to demonstrate how you can contribute to the current research program. There must then be space and resources to accommodate you. In this role, you may be acting as a professor's assistant, helping him or her conduct research for publication, as well as teaching undergraduate classes.

Many doctorate programs are either available in English or at least allow you to write your dissertation in English. Some programs charge tuition and others are free and include a living stipend. Doctorate programs in countries under the Bologna Process (a standardization of academic degrees across multiple countries) will generally last three years. However, those that earn their PhD under the Bologna Process will often do a post-doctorate degree of one or two more years if they want to remain in academia. The more traditional doctorate can last anywhere between four and seven years, depending upon the level of your responsibilities and the nature of your research. You may be considered an employee of the university rather than a student. While this has the advantage of being free of cost, you may not be granted student status and this has a number of implications. Namely, you'll need a different type of visa, not a student visa, and you won't be eligible for student discounts.

There is a lot of funding for PhD students wishing to conduct research at a university abroad, much more than what is available for potential bachelor's and master's students. Funding for a PhD usually comes in the form of a "fellowship," in which a student is given office space and other resources at a host institution, as well as a living stipend. In exchange, s/he must produce an article, a chapter of a book, a specific research agenda, or otherwise contribute to the goals of the institution. If you've reached the point in your education where you're considering a PhD, you are probably already familiar with the best universities in your subject matter. This can help you find a good program. You can also make use of the search engine www.gradschools.com, which allows you to search by either master's or PhD degrees, and by "international" programs.

Interest in a Particular Country

If you're considering college abroad at all, you probably have at least a passing interest in another language, culture, or country. Focusing on universities within your country or culture of interest is one way to narrow down your choices.

Some countries have websites that can answer the most fundamental questions about applying to university in that country. A student who did her master's in Norway found the website, www.studyinnorway.no, enormously helpful in answering her questions and finding the right program. If you find a website such as this one, make sure it is legitimate. The website should be run by or affiliated with the country's government or the regional accrediting body. If the website only lists private universities at the expense of public or national universities, it is probably for-profit. Some countries use a centralized, web-based application system that simultaneously enables you to apply to several universities within the target country. For example, if you want to study in Sweden you need to apply through the site www.universityadmissions.se and if you want to study in the UK you should apply through the Universities and Colleges Admissions Service, www.ucas.ac.uk

(only for undergraduates; prospective graduate students must apply directly to the program). These sites may charge a fee, similar to an application fee. Check with the admissions department in the country to make sure it's a legitimate process before paying anything through the website.

Even if you are interested in a certain country, be open-minded. If your goal is to study French literature or history, or become fluent in French, you don't have to limit your search to France. Additionally, consider Canada, Belgium, and Switzerland. There are also several Caribbean and African countries whose official language is French, where you will surely avoid the high cost of living in Paris.

Free or Low-Cost Education

Another way to narrow your search is by expense. If saving money is a goal, narrow your search to countries that have a strong tradition of free public education. This would include the majority of continental Europe, parts of Asia, South America, and Central America. Also, narrow your search primarily to "public" or "national" universities. These institutions depend almost entirely on state funds to operate, rather than tuition fees. Public and national universities abroad are often considered the best institutions in the country. Some don't charge tuition to international students, and some do.

While this is generally a good rule to follow, there are exceptions, such as the master's program I attended at Jacobs University in Germany, which is a private university that advertises its tuition at around $20,000 per year for undergraduate programs. The master's program, however, was free of charge. Similarly, the Korea Advanced Institute of Science and Technology, also a private organization, gives all its students full tuition waivers as long as they keep their grades at or above a "B" average. Another place to find reasonably priced international degree programs is through the Erasmus Mundus program, primarily located in EU countries. While many of these programs advertise that they charge tuition, they are heavily sponsored by a number of funding organizations, and there are numerous possibilities for scholarships covering not only tuition, but also living and sometimes travel expenses.

Tuition and fees aren't the only things to consider. While the University of Oslo doesn't charge tuition to any of its admitted students, Oslo is one of the most expensive cities in the world. So, narrow your search not only by countries or schools that charge low tuition rates, but also by cost-of-living standards.

Finally, you might want to limit your search to universities or countries that offer financial aid to international students. Regrettably, many countries that don't have a tradition of charging tuition also don't have a tradition of offering grants or scholarships. On the other hand, some countries are very interested in internationalization, and therefore offer a number of funding opportunities to international students. English-speaking countries especially are known to offer a variety of scholarships aimed at international students.

Finally, if you want to do college abroad, and you're willing to take out a student loan from the US government, you can limit your search to the universities abroad that are eligible for federal student loans. Get a complete list on the FAFSA website (www.fafsa.ed.gov).

7. Applying to a College Abroad

"It isn't necessary to imagine the world ending in fire or ice. There are two other possibilities: one is paperwork, and the other is nostalgia." —Frank Zappa

Now that you have found some programs, the next step is to dive head first into the sea of paperwork. If you've never applied to a university, the process may seem a bit overwhelming. Some institutions require you to apply directly to a degree program or school, even as an undergraduate student (such as the School of Humanities), while others will have you apply to the university, and still others will require you to apply through a nation-wide application system. The application process may be paper-based or electronic. The most important thing is to read the application materials *very* thoroughly, and to respect details and deadlines.

Although many educational systems operate on a similar academic calendar as the US, be mindful that some systems, particularly those south of the equator, may operate on a very different schedule. In Australia, New Zealand, and Brazil for example, the academic year starts in January. Schools in the Middle East tend to start in mid-October. Some countries and universities have rolling admissions, and may not even have application deadlines. If you're applying to schools in multiple countries, you'll have several different deadlines throughout the year, so be careful.

Previous Experience

You don't need previous time abroad to apply. When I applied to programs in Germany and Austria, the extent of my experience abroad was a trip to Mexico with my parents, a day (yes, only one day) in Canada on my way to Alaska, and a tour of Spain with my college choir. I wasn't exactly a world traveler, and yet I was admitted to many different overseas degree programs.

For very specialized programs in subjects like international law, universities may prefer time spent abroad. Apply anyway. You never know exactly what an admissions committee may be looking for, and something else on your application may stand out and replace the lack of experience abroad. State not only how the university can help you achieve your goals and aspirations, but also how you can contribute to the mission of the university.

Of course, if you do have extensive previous time overseas, don't hesitate to talk about these experiences in detail and how they influenced you to choose college abroad.

Grade Point Average

Grades aren't everything. Many US liberal arts colleges use detailed formulas that consider grades along with a multitude of other measures during the admissions process. They take into consideration extracurricular activities, but will also consider a student who didn't have time because she had to work. They pay a great deal of attention to motivation letters and essays, and I can say with much confidence that universities abroad do the same. They understand that good grades are not the only factor in determining good students. So whether you're in the 99th percentile of your high school class or the 50th, there is probably a college both in the US and abroad that will admit you.

Some institutions abroad may be more selective than the average American university. This may be the case when the country's high school students are achieving at a higher than average rate, and are therefore competitive candidates. On the other hand, some schools abroad may be less selective than the average American university. Don't leap to the conclusion that a more lenient selection process means a lower quality university. Keep in mind that institutions abroad approach admissions differently than US universities, and this might actually work in your favor.

GED vs. High School Diploma

Having a GED shouldn't hinder your ability to go to college abroad. Millions of people get their GED each year for a wide variety of understandable reasons. In fact, motivated high school students take the GED to complete high school early, in order to pursue uncommon paths afterwards—such as starting college early, or spending a year volunteering, traveling or studying abroad. While the test may have a negative stigma in the US, only those administrators abroad with intimate knowledge of the American educational system will have that same stigma. Many international students applying to school in the US use the GED as a way around the rather complicated process of getting transcripts translated and recognized in the US. If you're unsure if your college abroad will accept a GED, simply ask the admissions department.

College Admission Tests

Some foreign schools may require SAT or ACT scores, but most will not, unless you're applying to a joint or dual degree program administered by a US university. If you're applying to an "American-style" foreign university, you might expect to send SAT/ACT scores. If you're applying to graduate school, they may require GRE scores (or LSATs for law school, MCATs for medical school). But in my experience most foreign schools don't require test scores, especially if the program is designed to attract international students. Admissions boards simply can't interpret the scores from every national context. This could work to your advantage when applying to colleges abroad—while your friends and colleagues are stressing out over their SAT scores, you're brushing up on your Japanese.

On the other hand, if you're applying directly to an overseas public university, you may be required to submit scores from that country's admission test(s). This can be somewhat complicated, depending upon how and where the admission tests are conducted. Ask the international student office at the university if they have any knowledge or information about taking the tests from abroad. Maybe it is possible to take them online, or perhaps they are offered in some major US cities. Perhaps the university is willing to offer you a position contingent on getting a passing score on the exams, which you can do once you're in the country. In the worst-case scenario, you may have to fly to the destination country in question to take the test. While this could be expensive, it is also an opportunity to see the campus, check out the housing situation, meet professors and other current students, and of course, do some travel and sightseeing.

Letters of Recommendation

This should be the first thing you request when you start the application process, because you want to give your references plenty of time. The best people to ask for a recommendation letter are former or current teachers and professors. Ideally, it should be someone you have had for several classes, with whom you have a good working relationship. Another acceptable reference may be your counselor or advisor. You can also ask your employer for a recommendation, as long as you obtain at least one letter from someone who can speak about your academic qualities. You should not ask a friend or a family member.

In electronic applications, you may be asked to provide the email addresses of your references, and they will receive a link to an online recommendation form. Some institutions may have a specific form containing specific questions (either hard copy or electronic) and others may request an open-ended letter. Be sure to ask your references if they are willing and able to help you before putting their email addresses on the application form. You will probably be asking them for several letters—one for every institution to which you're applying. Tell them why you're applying to each program, and give them the college websites, so they can include specific details that match you to the program.

Be sure to read the instructions from each college carefully. A common requirement is to have the references place their letter inside of an envelope, seal it, and sign across the flap. Some may require that the letters be sent directly from your references, and not be included in your application packet. In this case, you should provide your references with pre-addressed and pre-stamped envelopes, but check to see if the postage is enough to arrive overseas.

To the extent that universities allow, I always recommend keeping application documents together for mailing purposes. For electronic applications, if the form is sent directly to the reference's email address, you won't need to worry about how to send the letter at all. In some cases, you might be asked to upload a copy to an online platform, which of course, requires you to open the letter and have it scanned. The university may require you to send a scanned version of the letter along with a hard copy in the mail.

Personal Statement

This may be the most difficult part of the application. Read the application form and follow the instructions precisely. Some universities will leave the statement completely up to your discretion. Others will ask for a "motivation letter," which is very similar to a cover letter you might write for a job application; you state your reasons for applying to the program and why you'd make a valuable contribution. Still other institutions may require something very particular—this may be true of programs with specific subject matter or student profile in mind.

Rather than allowing this part of the application to intimidate you, think of it as an excellent opportunity. It is your chance to illuminate certain qualities about yourself that aren't visible in the other application materials. I recommend looking at your resume or CV for things that may be very important but are missing. Work these missing qualifications into your personal statement. Also, re-emphasize things on your resume that make you a particularly attractive candidate. In your personal statement, you can give more specific details about what you did during an internship, for example. Include an explanation of why you want to go abroad for college. Also, show why your presence will make the program better—by contributing a small-town American perspective, for example.

Write your statement in a creative and interesting way, to make you stand out from the other applicants. Respect the length requirements as stated in the instructions—don't go over the page or word count. Finally, be sure to check the paper for grammar and spelling. It is always helpful to have someone else read your statement, like an academic counselor, a professor or a trusted peer, who can give you suggestions on how it sounds from a reader's perspective. If you're applying to a program in a non-native language, try to get a native or fluent speaker to read your essay and offer advice.

Research Proposal

Graduate programs will require more than a personal statement. For master's programs, you will probably have to state why you're interested in the subject matter, what sort of research you plan to do while in the program, how your research makes a contribution to the scientific community, and what sort of career aspirations you're working towards. For doctoral programs, you'll probably have to write a very extensive, heavily researched and well-sourced dissertation proposal. Research proposals vary in length from a brief five pages up to 30 or more. They usually include an outline of the research you hope to conduct, a timeline of how you will complete the project, how much the project will cost, where the money will come from, and an overview of the literature that has already been conducted in the field. Demonstrate how your research fits together with the philosophy and on-going research of the university or faculty group to which you're applying. See Peter Bentley's *The PhD Application Handbook,* for help on how to write an effective PhD research proposal.

Foreign Language Skills

If you're applying to a program conducted in English, you probably won't need to prove your English language skills. However, if the language of instruction is not English, you'll need to demonstrate your proficiency (unless of course your native language is the language of instruction at your college abroad). To prove your skills, you may need to take a test. The university should provide information about the tests and the minimum scores they accept for admission. Research the language test ahead of time. Find out what the test looks like, how long it takes, types of questions asked, the proportion that is written and how much is oral, how to best prepare, etc. There may be preparatory guides for these tests, similar to SAT prep books, available at your local bookstore or online. You will also need to know when, where, how often the test takes place, how to register for the test, and how much it costs. These tests may not take place often, and may be far away, so this part of the application process takes some advance planning. If you discover that you won't be able to take the test in time to make an application deadline, don't be afraid to ask the university if you can submit your scores later, even if after the deadline. Some universities may request an interview en lieu of formal test scores.

Resume or Curriculum Vitae

A resume is a standard requirement not only for college applications but also for job applications. Most high schools and colleges offer guidelines and classes on how to write an effective resume, and I encourage you to take advantage of these. Think of your resume as a series of "bullet points" by including only those things that are most relevant to your present application. Keep the length to one page, unless applying to a doctorate program, in which case it should be longer.

If you're applying to a university abroad, you may see the term "curriculum vitae" or "CV" rather than resume. They both serve the same purpose—to display your educational and employment history. Most employers and universities outside the US use the CV format. The CV is longer, gives more details, and contains additional sections on languages spoken, papers written, publications, scholarships, prizes won, soft skills, technological skills, hobbies, etc. If the application asks for a CV, you'll have to develop one based on your resume. If you are taking a class on resume writing, ask them about the CV as well.

Official Transcripts

Transcripts are the official list of classes you've taken, how many credit hours you earned from each class, and your final grade for each class, provided directly by your high school or university. You have to ask your institution in advance for the transcripts, and you may have to pay for them. Your college abroad may require that your previous school send them directly, or it may simply require that the transcript come in a sealed envelope, with the signature of an administrator or the official school seal across the flap.

Most schools have streamlined processes to fulfill transcript requests, just be sure to provide specific instructions, with the general request. Order several copies at once—and order one or two extra copies beyond the number you think you'll need (trust me, you'll need them). Be sure, however, to keep them sealed in the envelope, as many colleges won't accept transcripts out of the envelope. If you're applying using an online platform, you may be asked to open the envelope and scan the document; you may also be asked to provide the original sealed transcripts at a later date. If you're applying before you've graduated, the transcript should indicate that you're expected to graduate on a certain date with a certain standing. The transcript should also include a list of the classes that you're currently taking, and an indication that these classes will fulfill any requirements that are left for you to successfully graduate.

Diplomas

If you're applying to an undergraduate program directly out of high school, you may need a copy of your high school diploma. If you're applying to a graduate program, similarly you'll need to provide a copy of your bachelor's and/or master's diploma. If you haven't graduated yet, you can submit transcripts in lieu of a diploma. In this case, you might be given a "conditional" acceptance, which means that you're accepted to the program under the provision that you will provide proof of a degree before you begin.

Because you'll be sending photocopies, some institutions will require that you get them officially notarized. Notaries are usually available at the post office and major banks. They charge a small fee for their services, and may require that you photocopy the degree in his/her presence, so s/he can be sure it is authentic. Make several copies, as you never know how many you'll need. The notary will stamp and sign the copy officially. The copy that you send to the university has to be the copy with an original stamp and signature from the notary. Not all universities will require that you provide a notarized copy. Some universities may only require it for international students, because it is difficult for them to validate your degree from afar.

Academic Writing Sample

This is relatively simple and is probably more relevant for those applying to a graduate rather than an undergraduate program. Pick an essay you've written previously for class, one that makes you proud. It's even better if the topic is connected to the subject matter of the program to which you're applying. Make a copy of it, and put it with your application materials. Reread it beforehand and make any necessary edits. If you're applying to an undergraduate program and you don't have a workable writing sample, ask your college what is acceptable in lieu of previous academic work. You may have to write something as if you were writing for a class. In this case, ask your favorite teacher to give you an essay "assignment." Have him or her determine the basic requirements and the general topic. Write the essay, and allow the teacher to grade it (and maybe you can even ask for extra credit).

Translations

If you're applying to a program conducted in another language, you may need your documents translated. However, be sure to read the application instructions carefully; English documents may be acceptable since English is so widely spoken. If translated documents are required, you have one of two options. The first option is to have your documents professionally translated using someone from a translation company that can provide an official certification. The second option allows you to translate your own documents and then have the translation certified by a professional translator. However, you should only attempt the second option if you're fluent in the language. Send the originals along with the translations and certifications all together.

Application Form

The application forms can usually be downloaded from the university's website, or completed online. You might need to register with the university's online application system, in which case you'll receive a username and password. The online application procedure may allow you to complete the process in stages by logging in, saving your progress, and then logging out and in again until you're finished. In some cases, you may not be able to stop the process, so be sure you have everything you need before starting. Fill it out as honestly and as completely as possible, and follow the instructions closely. If you have questions about some information that is required on the form, don't be afraid to get in touch with the admissions office. If you're using a paper form, write and sign clearly.

Interview

Colleges abroad may or may not require an interview. Interviews are more common for master's and PhD programs. Fortunately, modern technology makes interviewing easy and cheap, with online voice and video applications such as Skype. For my admissions process, I used Skype (a free voice-over-internet application). You'll need to download the application, create an account, and if your computer doesn't have a built-in microphone, you'll need to purchase one. Of course, the university may opt for a good old-fashioned phone interview, OR in rare cases you'll be required to do an interview in person. If they require an interview in person, they will probably offer funding to pay for the airfare. When scheduling an interview, pay close attention to the time difference—it may require you to stay up somewhat late or get up very early so that the university can contact you during their normal working hours.

Interviews can be nerve-racking, but there are plenty of guidebooks on how to prepare. My advice is to be yourself and answer the questions honestly. If you're applying for a doctorate position, the bulk of the interview will probably be spent on questions regarding your research proposal. The interviewers may purposefully try to find something in your project that you've overlooked. If you don't know the answer to a question, don't be afraid to admit this openly and thank the interviewers for pointing it out—their goal is probably to help you make your proposal stronger as well as get to know you better and how you handle pressure. See the interview also as an opportunity for you to ask questions about the university, program, or a specific professor you hope to work with later on.

Application Fee

If there is an application fee, you may have to wire the funds from your bank account in the United States. This is the safest and most reliable way to move money across borders, especially if the amount is significant. The fees to wire money internationally can be somewhat high if you do it directly from a bank (on average between $30 and $50). There are some third party companies that can handle the trade for a considerably smaller fee, depending upon the currencies being traded and the method of deposit (see XE Trade www.xe.com). The university may alternatively accept a credit card number or PayPal. Check with your credit card company to find out what fees they charge and compare this with the fees charged by PayPal and a wire transfer company like Western Union or XE Trade. Sometimes fees, even for a small amount, can be quite high if you don't shop around. Also, find out if the application fee is refundable, just in case you're not accepted or if you don't accept a position.

Identifying Documents

As a foreigner applying to college abroad, you may be required to submit a copy of your passport along with the application materials. If you don't have a passport yet, begin the application process immediately! Contact the college and ask if you can send a copy of your passport later (if you think you won't get it before the deadline), or ask if they'll accept a copy of your state ID or driver's license instead, at least until you get a passport.

Submit your Application

Now that you've compiled all the materials, put them in a large envelope and take it to the post office. You'll be presented with all kinds of options for sending mail internationally—express, insured, delivery confirmation, etc. All of this is up to you, but the most important thing is to make sure it arrives on time. Check the application form regarding the deadline and make sure you're sending your application with enough advance time. Confirm with the Post Office the estimated time of delivery for your package. Many universities have come to understand that mail delivery—particularly international mail delivery—can be unpredictable. This is why they may have a "postmark" deadline instead of an "arrival" deadline. This means the postmark must show that you sent the envelope on or before the deadline. Note, if you bring your envelope to the post office the day of the deadline, it may not be postmarked until the next day.

Now the waiting game begins. You've said "yes" to college abroad, and now it is time to hear "yes" back.

8. Getting Ready to Go

"Kilometers are shorter than miles. Save gas, take your next trip in kilometers." —George Carlin

"Yes! And..."

Congratulations! You've fought half the battle of going to college abroad. By now, you've probably been accepted to several different universities, and it's time to make a decision. The first step now is simple—say "yes!" Most universities will want you to formally accept their offer by a certain deadline. If you have to sign something, read it carefully as there might be certain requirements you have to fulfill. The university may require a non-refundable deposit in order to secure your place. The deposit may be a one-off payment, or it may be used towards student fees once you arrive. There's a lot to do before you leave. This chapter will help you prepare for your departure.

Do your Research

You already did some research when you found the college and decided to apply, but now you can take a deeper look at the country and what you're likely to encounter. A lot of this general information is available for free on the Internet. Be mindful, however, of the source. You may also consider reading popular books and news from that country, to glean some insight into the views and values of the culture you're about to join. Having knowledge of current events is also a good way to show your soon-to-be friends that you're interested in them and their culture.

It's especially important to familiarize yourself with the metric system, the local currency, and the exchange rate, for practical purposes. When you're at the store, try to envision how many liters are in that gallon of milk or how many grams are in a can of beans. When you're driving, think about the distance in kilometers instead of miles. Think also in terms of Celsius instead of Fahrenheit. If you really want a challenge, as well as a great intercultural perspective, look up the current gas prices in your host country, per liter and in local currency. To know how that translates to dollars per gallon, you'll have to do several conversions at once.

Passport

Having a passport is your ticket to the world. If you already have a passport, then you may be able to skip this section, but check the expiration date first. If it is expiring within the year, you should get a new one before you leave. If it will expire while you're living overseas, you'll have to renew it at the American embassy in your host country. All of the information you need to get a passport is on the State Department's website: travel.state.gov. Start the process early. It can take several weeks just to put together all the required documentation, and after you submit your application, it can take several weeks (or more) to receive your passport. There are procedures in place if you need to rush the application, but I highly recommend just giving yourself enough time. Rushing your application is quite expensive and increases the likelihood that something will go wrong.

Download the passport application form from the website, and follow the instructions carefully. Any minor mistake or oversight can cause significant delays, and your application fee is nonrefundable even if your application is rejected. When your paperwork is complete and you have all the documentation, take it to a nearby passport agency. You can find this information on the website. Don't sign the application form

80

until you are instructed to do so by the agent. If it's the first time you are applying, you will need to appear in person.

You'll need to provide official government-issued proof of American citizenship. These include an official and original (not a photocopy!) birth certificate from the state in which you were born, proof of birth abroad, a naturalization certificate, or other citizenship certification. A state-issued ID or driver's license is NOT enough. If you don't have your birth certificate (and this is actually quite common so don't panic), the state, city or county should have a record of your birth, and they can produce a new certificate. Oftentimes, this certificate has to be signed by a notary to be considered official. You'll also need your social security number.

In addition, you will have to present another proof of identity, which can be a driver's license, a government-issued ID card, a naturalization certificate, or a military ID. The type of identification you choose to submit must be current. You will also need to bring a copy of all the above forms of identification.

Be prepared to pay the passport fee at the acceptance agency. Unfortunately, passports are expensive but they are usually valid for 10 years. The fees seem to change constantly, so check the website for the most up to date information. Cash is not accepted so bring your credit card or checkbook.

You will also need to bring TWO passport photos. The photos must fulfill very specific requirements and dimensions. Many photo studios, post offices, and even drug stores (I had my photos taken at a Walgreens) are aware of these guidelines. Still, I recommend reading the requirements ahead of time and making sure your photographer is aware of them before you proceed. Passport photos can be somewhat expensive so you want to make sure they are right the first time. Although you only need two photos for your passport, I strongly recommend that you get a package of 10 photos or so. There are a number of instances where having passport photos are useful, including additional ID cards abroad, visas, residence permits and job applications.

Once you receive your passport, immediately put it in a safe place, but also a place that is easily accessible. If leaving soon, you won't want your passport stashed in a safe deposit box. I recommend getting a passport wallet for safekeeping, which also comes in handy when traveling. Make several copies of your passport and put them in a safe place as well. Leave one with someone you trust who will stay in the US while you're abroad, and keep one with you in a different place than the actual passport. You'll need a copy if you lose your passport and need to apply for a new one. Sign on the appropriate page in the passport, and fill in the emergency contact information (in pencil, so you can change it if necessary).

Student Visa and/or Residence Permit

Every country has slightly different requirements in terms of the documentation you need to travel, study, live or work. Check the website of the country's embassy in the United States, the State Department's website (travel.state.gov), and cross-reference these sources with the information provided to you by the university's international student office. There is a drop down menu on the State Department's website where you may choose the destination country. From there, scroll down to "Entry and Exit Regulations." Sometimes, the country does not require a US student to obtain a visa beforehand. Most countries participating in the Visa Waiver Program fall into this category. This means that you may be able to enter the country with only your passport, and then later obtain a residence permit from local authorities, usually within three months of arriving.

When looking at the embassy website, you will quickly discover there are many different types of visas and residence permits. Be sure to look specifically at the information for students (unless you'll be an employee of the university as a PhD candidate, in which case you'll need a different visa); you may not need a visa to enter the country, or you may need to apply for a residence permit ahead of time. Although visas and residence permits are different documents, for the purposes of this chapter I'll refer to "visa" as a general term for either a formal student visa or a residence permit. The documents you will need in order to get either of these will be similar.

Because you'll probably need an admission letter from the university in order to obtain a visa, you can't begin the application process until you've been accepted. Collecting the documents you need for a visa will take some time, so it's good to allow yourself extra time anyway. Below is a sample of the documentation you *might* need for a visa application. It is a good idea to take these items with you to college abroad, even if you don't need them for a visa. You might end up needing them to get a residence permit or for other formalities with the university. You should also consider leaving a copy of all these important documents with someone you trust back home.

- **Application form**. Either download from the embassy's website or pick up at the consulate.

- **Passport and photocopies.**

- **Passport-sized photos.** If the country to which you're applying for a visa has different regulations and dimension requirements for their photos than American passport photos, you'll need to get different photos taken. Requirements are probably on the application forms or the embassy's website. Make sure whoever is taking the photos understands that the dimensions are different from the American passport photos.

- **Proof of your address in the US**. Even if you plan to live overseas for a long period of time, you'll want to keep a "permanent address" in the US where you can receive mail. To prove your address in the US, you will need to provide something like a driver's license or a utility bill in your name with the address on it.

- **Copy of birth certificate or other official proof of citizenship.**

- **Copies of your parents' passports or their proof of citizenship**.

- **Emergency contact information**. I recommend using a relative who will remain in the US during your entire stay, someone who is reliable and accessible.

- **Official admission letter from the university, and perhaps copies thereof.**

- **Proof of finances**. The embassy will be specific about what they need to see in order to process your visa application. For a student visa, they may need to see a bank account statement showing a certain minimal amount of money that you will need to support yourself while living in the country. If you're receiving a scholarship, grant or loan, you'll need to provide an official letter from the funding institute stating how much you'll be receiving.

- **Medical records**. Some countries require proof that you've received certain vaccinations, a note from a doctor after having gone through a general checkup, proof of blood type, and particularly in the case of African countries, proof that you haven't been exposed to HIV/AIDS. Of course, in order to provide these documents, you'll probably have to make an appointment with your doctor beforehand. There may be a specific form that needs to be filled out by a qualified medical professional.

- **Proof of health insurance.** Most countries require that you have acceptable health insurance to get a visa. You won't be able to provide proof of this until you're in the country and have applied for coverage, so this requirement is typical of visas or residence permits you obtain after entering the country. You'll need to show an official letter from the insurance company or national health service, or a copy of your enrollment card.

- **Self-addressed stamped envelope**. In some cases, the embassy can process the visa request the same day; however, usually they will take your passport, paste the visa onto one of the pages, and mail it back to you in the envelope you provide. A consulate is a smaller branch of the embassy where routine procedures such as visa applications take place. It is meant to serve those living outside the Washington DC area. You might be able to pick up your visa and passport directly from the embassy/consulate, rather than waiting for it in the mail.

- **Application fee**. Be sure to check with the embassy about what forms of payment they accept. The fee is usually nonrefundable.

- **Appearance at the embassy**. In most cases, you have to appear in person at the embassy or consulate to present your passport and application. If you don't live near Washington DC, there will probably be a consulate that has jurisdiction over the area of the US in which you reside. If you apply over the Internet, the service is probably being handled by a third party, in which case the fees may be higher.

Before you throw up your hands at this rather long list of documents, understand that it isn't any easier for international students to study in the United States. The process to obtain a student visa to study in the US is so time-consuming and laborious that there are several private companies that a student can hire to help them. Furthermore, even when the visa has been successfully obtained, arriving students may still be denied entry by immigration authorities.

Entry or Transit Visas

Once you begin to make your flight arrangements, you may need to think about other types of visas beyond the student visa for your final destination. If you have several stops along the way, each country in which you land may also require a visa. Entry visas are usually valid for a short period, but allow you to enter the country beyond the airport. Transit visas, on the other hand, typically only allow you to land in that country's airport on your way to somewhere else. These visas are usually easier to obtain, and in some cases they can actually be obtained directly at the airport. An American requires a visa when entering Turkey for example, but the visa only amounts to standing in a special line, paying a small fee (they even accept US dollars), and having the visa stamped into your passport before you go through immigration. If you land in any country without the proper visa, you can be immediately sent back to the US at your own expense, and you may also face lengthy questioning by the local authorities. Note that many countries do not require a visa for American citizens. Also note that if you've already traveled, in rare circumstances you might be denied entry to certain destinations if you have stamps from countries that aren't friendly with your destination. For example, if you have stamps from Israel, you may be denied entry into certain Arab countries. All of this information should be noted on the State Department and the embassy websites.

International Ticket

Airfare pricing doesn't always make sense, but there are some general guidelines you can use to find low fares. The best days to fly are usually Tuesday and Wednesday. The cheapest flights typically leave early in the morning or very late at night, and include a Saturday stay-over. Begin searching at least four months in advance; flights purchased too far in advance are usually expensive as well as flights purchased at the last minute. It is sometimes possible to find last minute deals, but I wouldn't risk waiting and hoping for a deal only to pay an outrageous price. Flexibility can also help, and since you're moving abroad, you'll be more flexible than the average tourist. You can readily take the flight that arrives four weeks before university orientation, for example. If so, you can use the extra time to find a place to live and settle in. In some cases, flying to a smaller airport will save you money because large airports charge carriers high fees. You may be able to fly to another city for much less and take a train to your final destination.

Be flexible about potential stopovers. Iceland Air began offering extremely competitive airfare from select US cities to Europe, with a stopover in Reykjavik, after their epic economic crash.

Finally, since you're moving abroad you may be tempted to look for one-way flights, but for some strange reason round-trip fare is often (but not always) more economical than a one-way ticket. Although the airlines don't like it, you may want to buy a round-trip ticket and then simply fail to show up to your return flight. Therefore, search for both one-way and round-trip fares.

Set up a price alert for your connection. Many websites offer this service, but I like Kayak (www.kayak.com) the best. You tell the website your destination and origination and the approximate dates you want to fly, and it will search for the best prices, and send you an email when they find something that fits your criteria. Bing's travel predictor (bing.com/travel) shows you the probability of a flight going up or down in price, if the connection is popular. By setting up a price alert, you get a good idea of the average price, and you will be among the first to know if it drops.

If the price drops one day, go to the website and play around with the dates to see if flying earlier or later is better. Before you leap and buy, check other flight aggregators, too, like Skyscanner and Momondo, because the airlines searched by every aggregator differ slightly. Then, go to the airline's website and see if the flight is cheaper to buy direct. Sometimes this saves you money. Keep in mind that most carriers don't include baggage and other fees in their advertised fare. Just when you think you've scored an amazing deal, and start booking, the fees start adding up. Most aggregators like Kayak attempt to quote you the final, total price of the flight including baggage fees and taxes in the initial search. Fortunately, most major carriers include the first piece of checked luggage on international flights for free.

When you purchase your flight, you'll have the opportunity to put in a frequent flier number. Even if you don't plan on flying much during your stay abroad, it is still worth it to join the frequent flier program of the major carrier between your host country and home. Major airlines are clustered in networks, so even if you don't fly that specific airline all the time, you can still earn miles on flights with other airlines in the same network. If you've already been earning frequent flier miles, consider using your miles to pay for your initial flight overseas or upgrade to a higher class (a higher class may give you an additional checked bag for free).

Financial Arrangements

How you manage your money while abroad will depend on how you finance your stay. If you're receiving funding from an institution based in the United States, you'll need to work out how the money will be disbursed. Perhaps they can send it to your account abroad, or perhaps they can only disburse it to a US account. If financing your stay through personal savings, you can wire money from your US account to your account abroad. Don't forget about the fees for international wires I mentioned earlier, as well as some of the third party companies that charge less than banks. However, you won't be able to do this until after you arrive and have set up your local bank account. In the meantime, use your ATM card for taking small amounts of money from your account in the US.

If possible, try to consolidate your money into one or two accounts before you leave. This will make it easier for you to manage from overseas. The more money you have in a high-yield savings account, the more interest it will earn. Choose a major bank with partnerships abroad to avoid paying unnecessary fees. Banking online with paperless statements will be the easiest way to manage your accounts from abroad, pay bills at home, and move money between accounts. If you connect the accounts through inter-institution online transfers, and choose banks that allow you to transfer money for free, you can easily move money whenever you need.

For your bank in the US, it's a good idea to find one with branches near your permanent address. This means that when you go home to visit, you'll be able to go to the bank in person and deposit grandma's birthday check or withdraw dollars. It's a good idea to give someone you trust access to your account so that s/he can take care of certain issues while you're away (e.g. depositing checks). When my parents occasionally gave me money, they would simply deposit it into a joint account that we set up near their house in Colorado. I could see online when they made a deposit.

The easiest and cheapest way to move small amounts of money across international borders is to withdraw cash from ATM machines. PayPal is an option, but beware of the fees they charge. To avoid ATM withdrawal fees, you'll need to do some research. Figure out how the ATMs operate in your host country and whether or not your current ATM card will work overseas. Some countries have ATM machines that require 5 digit PIN codes, or require access codes that contain letters. If your code does not comply with these requirements, you won't be able to use it in these ATMs. Typically if you use an ATM card at a machine in the same network, the fees are more reasonable. Some banks even waive their fees if you fulfill certain criteria. You probably won't need to use your ATM card much overseas because you'll have a local bank account.

Credit cards may not be widely used in your host country. Therefore, don't plan to use them regularly. You can either use cash or your local debit card to make day-to-day purchases. However, for some large purchases (like airfare home) and purchases online, you may still use your credit card. It's a good idea to call your credit card company before you leave and let them know where you'll be living and for how long, otherwise your card may be blocked for security reasons when you try to use it. Do the same with your ATM card. If you plan to use your cards while traveling outside of your host country, update your banks with these plans as well. Choose a card that has no annual fee and includes either a travel rewards program or a cash back program. This way, you can earn miles towards a vacation flight or cash to help you finance your stay. You can also look for a credit card that includes other complimentary travel-related services, like insurance coverage for lost luggage and delayed flights.

Next, think about taxes. Taxes are a rather complicated issue for Americans living abroad, so it is worth investigating your specific situation ahead of time. Peruse the IRS's website, or consult a tax attorney if your situation is particularly complex. IRS publication 54 ("Tax Guide for United States Citizens and Resident Aliens Abroad") is very helpful in this regard. Unfortunately, the United States is one of the few countries in the world that attach taxation to citizenship rather than residency. What this means is that as an American, you can be double taxed for income earned abroad, by both the US and the country in which the income was earned. However, if your total income is less than a certain limit, you're not obligated to file a tax return at all. Any interest you pay on existing student loan debt qualifies for a deduction, but if you put your loan into deferment you won't qualify.

E-filing is common and secure for overseas filers. If filing electronically, be sure to bring with you any important documents you'll need, like W2's from the previous year. If you can't or won't file electronically, you have a few options. You can appoint someone ahead of time to file your taxes (such as your Power of Attorney), you can visit an international US tax office in your host country, or you can do your taxes on paper and mail them to the US. More information can be found on the IRS's website.

Internet Calls

The Internet has revolutionized how people communicate and has made it incredibly easy and cheap to do so across international borders, as long as you have a computer and an Internet connection. Most new laptops come with an internal microphone and an integrated webcam, but if you're planning to use a computer abroad that doesn't have these features, then you'll need to buy the external components before you leave. These components may not be easily found in your host country or might be very expensive.

There are several applications that allow international users to talk for free. My favorite is Skype, but there are alternatives such as VoxOx and Google Voice. Skype-to-Skype calls are completely free. In addition, for a very reasonable fee, you can purchase a Skype phone number that acts as a landline. Having this number is incredibly useful. You can choose the area code from where the number will originate, such as your permanent address in the US, or from wherever your most important contacts in the US will be calling. This means that businesses, your credit card company, and your friends and family will be able to call you at a local number, which rings through to your Skype account. If you're not online when they call, you can have the call forwarded to your local cell phone or landline number, which costs a small fee. If the caller is still unable to reach you, Skype includes an integrated voicemail service. To the person on the other end of the line, it will seem as if you're sitting in your home answering the phone in

Anytown, USA. If you need to call someone in the US from your host country, the rates using online applications like Skype are very cheap, and calling 1-800 numbers on Skype is free. Work with friends or family that are less internet-savvy to set up Skype on their computers before you leave. Internet-based chat and voice applications are also useful for communicating with local friends you make while living abroad.

Cell phones and SIM cards

It is important to think about how you will communicate in your host country. Most people throughout the world use cell phones. For your current cell phone to work abroad, it must be "unlocked" (untethered from the SIM card with which it was sold) so that it will work with another SIM card. SIM cards are the small chips that are inserted into cell phones that allow the phone to communicate with the mobile network. The phone must also be a tri- or quad-band, which means it recognizes and operates on wireless networks abroad. The United States uses a type of wireless network that isn't common in other parts of the world, although some carriers are beginning to use the more international networks. If the phone isn't tri- or quad-band, it won't work abroad, even if it is unlocked. Check your phone model to know for sure. Ask your carrier to unlock your phone. Show them proof you're moving abroad and they may unlock it for free and let you out of your contract without paying a cancellation fee. If you're still in contract, it is more difficult to get out of it and get the phone unlocked, but it is not impossible. If you can't get your phone unlocked, it will be useless to you abroad. In this case, sell your phone online or consider donating it (domestic battery shelters take old phones for women to use in emergencies).

If you need an unlocked phone, you can buy an inexpensive phone and SIM card that will work abroad. This is usually much more cost-effective than buying a cell phone and signing a contract with a monthly fee. I recommend getting one that is made especially for your host country, rather than a traveler's card that works in multiple countries. You'll be spending most of your time in your host country, and the cards that work within a country have the most competitive rates. SIM cards come with a certain dollar amount preloaded, and there are a number of different ways you can add more minutes to the card, such as through the Internet with your credit card or by purchasing "top-up" codes from local stores.

You can arrange to buy a cell phone and local SIM card when you get to your host country, but I recommend getting an unlocked phone and SIM card before you leave, so that you have a way of communicating as soon as you land. You might need to call a host family or the university when you arrive. If you find a SIM card in your host country with better rates, you can simply use the card you purchased in the US until you've run out of credit, and then buy a new one. SIM cards and unlocked cell phones can be purchased through sites like Telestial (www.telestial.com) and shipped to your address in the US before you leave. You can also purchase SIM cards that work in the US so you can use your unlocked phone when you're back for a visit.

Register with the State Department

Although not essential, you might consider registering with the US State Department's Smart Traveler Enrollment Program, as an American expatriate living abroad. The registration is free and simple, and can be done directly through the travel section of the website (travel.state.gov). Once registered, the State Department will send you travel warnings or alerts for a specific country, and they'll have your emergency contact information in case something happens. While you're on their website, print the addresses and phone number of the American embassy and consulates in your host country and keep that information with you. You may also want to leave this information with someone you trust back home.

Health Insurance

Now that you're going abroad, think about how you'll be covered for medical care and emergencies. Can you remain on your parents' plan while living overseas? Is health insurance in your host country required or not? What are the options? What is the cost? Do your research by asking current students and searching the Internet. Even if you can remain on your parents' plan, it may actually be cheaper to be insured locally, with less hassle and paperwork. If you plan to remain on your parents' insurance, confirm that you'll have international coverage, and if so, ask for an official verification letter.

There may be both "public" and "private" health insurance plans, but these words are misleading. Look into the advantages and disadvantages of each so you'll be prepared to make the right decision once you arrive. For example, in Germany, the public plans are slightly more expensive than the private plans, but the public plans cover nearly everything while the private plans are more restrictive. The private plans require customers to pay for treatment upfront, and then seek reimbursement later. By contrast, the public plans require little to no out-of-pocket expenses beyond the monthly premium. Additionally, the law doesn't allow those covered in the private network to change at will to the public plan. This means that if you choose a private insurance company, you're stuck with that decision for the duration of your studies. The more research you do ahead of time, the better decision you'll make.

In addition to gathering information about the local health insurance plans, you may also want to take care of a few health-related issues with your US doctor before you leave. Remember that you may need a general medical report or vaccinations for your visa application. If you're going to a country that requires specific vaccinations, you'll probably want to bring an International Certification of Vaccinations from the World Health Organization. This is an internationally recognized document showing that you are vaccinated. It may make it easier for you to get a visa and get through immigration at the airport. You may also want to identify some English-speaking doctors in the city where you'll be living. Even in non-English speaking countries, there are probably doctors who speak English and were trained in an English-speaking environment.

Beyond routine examinations, you might ask your US doctor about any specific conditions you have and how to navigate this in your host country. Ask your doctor about the availability of your prescriptions, and familiarize yourself with what your condition is called in the local language. Get any prescriptions refilled before you leave so you have time to figure out how to refill them abroad. Be sure to keep the medicine in its original, labeled container when you go through security and customs at the airport.

Women should ask also about birth control, whether contraceptives will be available in the host country, and how to visit an Ob/Gyn. If your doctor doesn't have the answers, she can at least guide you to the right resources. Get as many birth control pills as possible before you leave.

Write up a document that includes all of your basic health care information such as blood type, allergies, specific conditions or major surgeries you've had, prescription drugs you're on, and emergency contact information (your medical bio sheet). If possible, have it translated into the local language. Keep this document with you in your wallet, and leave one with a trusted person back home.

Ask a local student or the university about dental coverage and eye care in the host country. These services may not be covered with your local insurance scheme, in which case you might consider seeing your dentist and optometrist before you leave and when you return home for visits. On the other hand, even if local insurance won't cover these things, the out-of-pocket expenses for these services may be very inexpensive in your host country. If you wear glasses or contacts, make sure your prescription is current and consider getting new glasses or contact lenses before you leave.

Check with your college or current students if the local health insurance will cover you outside your host country. Some insurance will cover you with some minor modifications, and others simply don't cover you if you get sick while traveling. If your insurance won't cover you while outside your host country, consider getting additional traveler's insurance. You'll also want to know that you're covered when you go back to the US for a short-term visit. There are a few insurance plans on the market that are designed for expatriates and long-term travelers. I use TripPlus (www.tripplus.com), which is a very bottom-dollar insurance plan for travelers (and I've never had occasion to make a claim). It certainly isn't full medical coverage, but for only $75 a year, it is worth it to me because I try to travel as much as possible while living abroad.

Renewals

Plan to renew your driver's license and credit cards before you leave if they are expiring soon. Even if you're not planning to drive abroad, you will probably need to drive when you go home for visits. You will need your credit cards for emergencies or for large purchases.

You may also wish to get an International Driving Permit from AAA. Should you need to communicate with foreign authorities, this familiar form of identification can help a lot. It's valid in over 150 countries and contains your name, photo, and driver's information translated into ten languages. Bring an application, a valid United States driver's license, $15 (current fee), and two original passport-type photos, to an AAA office nearby.

Legal Will

Especially if you're young, writing a will may be the farthest thing from your mind. It isn't a necessity, but if you have a lot of assets in the US, or have instructions for your family should anything happen to you, it's a good idea. If you don't have complicated requests, there are free, simple forms online that you can fill in with your information. Although the regulations vary from state to state, generally a simple will needs to be signed by two witnesses in the presence of a notary as well as yourself. They should be trusted people in your life, but they CANNOT be people that are named as beneficiaries in the will, as that would cause a conflict of interest. Get several copies of the will signed and notarized, and leave a copy with the executor of the will (the person that you put in charge of managing your assets upon death).

You may also want to consider writing up a power of attorney. A power of attorney gives a certain individual you trust absolute authority over your assets, bank accounts, and any other property should something happen to you and you can't make decisions for yourself. Doing so makes managing your money and property easier for the person you put in charge, even if you're fully conscious and healthy overseas. I gave my parents power of attorney before I went abroad, even though I had no significant assets to manage. It ended up being helpful

95

because it allowed them to open and close a few bank accounts in my name without me having to go home.

A living will, also called an advanced directive, is a list of detailed instructions for what you want your family to do in case you become so severely ill or injured that you aren't able to make your own medical decisions. You can give your loved ones instructions regarding under what circumstances you'd like to remain on life support and when you'd like to be taken off. You can make your wishes known verbally to your family, but nothing is legally binding unless you put your wishes down on paper and get it notarized. A properly signed and notarized will and power of attorney will cover procedures in the United States. However, if you are overseas, your medical rights are subject to the laws in your host country, which may not respect the wishes outlined in your advanced directive. In any case, you should bring a copy of all these documents with you and once overseas, put them in a safe place. After you've established some relationships with people you trust, let someone know where these documents are in case something happens to you.

Safekeeping Important Information

Copies of your passport and student visa, original notarized and signed copies of your will and other legal documents, and a detailed health history, should all be left with someone at home for safekeeping. Additionally, it's a good idea to leave copies of your travel insurance card, credit cards, ATM cards, driver's license and other identifications, acceptance letters to the university, high school and college transcripts, and original diplomas.

I also recommend creating an emergency contact sheet with important information that you can leave with someone back home and keep for yourself. Include the following:

- Contact information for someone at the university, ideally your program coordinator
- Contact information for any other locals you'll be relying upon, such as a current student or host family
- Phone number and address of the hotel, hostel, or

person you'll be staying with before securing your own accommodation
- The phone number and address of the American Embassy and Consulates
- The address and phone number of the local police, if you can find it online beforehand
- Local emergency numbers (the equivalent of 911)

Packing

You've collected documents, gone through the arduous application process, gotten your passport, and even purchased an airline ticket. Now you have to pack and get on the plane! Since you are packing for all four seasons, and you won't be coming home any time soon, you will need to plan carefully. Packing for a move abroad requires a different strategy than your parents' three-week getaway to Europe and your older sister's semester abroad. Once you start condensing your life into a couple of suitcases, reality sets in. Everyone's packing list will be somewhat different, but these basic guidelines should help get you started.

If you're anything like me, compacting your entire life into a couple of suitcases has a way of taking you down memory lane as you evaluate every item and its worthiness of the journey. High school graduates going to college anywhere away from home will experience a similar emotional process, especially if it is their first time. The process of packing may bring up some doubts and hesitation, through the sneaky little voice that wants to convince you to stay home. It wants you to say, "No, I can't do this!", "I'll never fit everything in my bags", "What if I forget something", or "What if I don't need x or y."

Many self-help books recommend reevaluating your life occasionally and shedding unnecessary and frivolous items. Things you've collected over many years that seem somehow important may actually be weighing you down. Packing can help you reassess your values and begin the process of opening your mind to a new culture and lifestyle. It is also an excellent opportunity to go through your belongings and get rid of things you don't use or need anymore. When I got rid of things before moving abroad, I thought I'd feel empty and sad, but in fact I ended up feeling a sense of power and freedom. This process may be emotional, but it's important to keep things in perspective.

You might be wondering why I haven't mentioned shipping things to your new home. This is certainly an option, and many people who are moving abroad for a job will choose to ship their items, thanks to relocation assistance. But if you're trying to move abroad on a budget, you should know that shipping internationally is extremely expensive. Financially, it makes more sense to take an additional checked bag on the flight rather than ship a box. The general guideline for international flights in economy class is that you get one free checked bag with a maximum weight of 50 pounds. A second checked bag costs around $50, also with a limit of 50 pounds. Compare this to a large box with a weight limit of 20 pounds to Europe at $75, or a package with a weight of 50 pounds at $200! Furthermore, when you ship large boxes overseas they are subject to intense inspection by customs authorities. Not to mention, shipping is difficult if you don't know where you'll be living.

Think of other ways to get your belongings overseas without paying for shipping. Consider when the next time it is you'll be coming home. If your academic year starts in September, perhaps you may be thinking of coming home for the holidays only a few months later. Therefore, you might be able to get away with only one checked item for your initial move, and then bring the rest of your items when you come back from the holidays. Maybe you have a worried parent who wants to come with you when you move, or come visit you only shortly after you arrive. Take advantage of this and pack some things in your parent's checked bag.

Try to pack light. You can justify a second bag for an extra fee, but if you find yourself considering a third or fourth bag, take a step back. Once you've laid out all the items you want to take with you, divide the pile in half and take only the half. Remember that whatever you put on the plane will need to be transported from the airport. As a student, your wardrobe will probably be fairly casual. Also, you'll probably purchase at least a few items abroad, to fit into the local fashion. Therefore, you don't need to bring everything you own.

Remember that besides your carry-on and checked luggage, you also can bring items with you on your person. Think strategically about what to actually wear on the plane. You'll want to be comfortable for the long flight, but you'll also want to be prepared for the climate upon arrival. When I go on a long overseas flight, I dress in layers for two reasons. I can bring more with me without adding to the weight of my bags and I can also be prepared for a variety of climates and temperatures (and I always get very cold on a plane). I wear shoes or boots that would be difficult to pack. I usually wear a jacket as well, because jackets are difficult to pack.

Finally, start the packing process early. Start laying out items at least a week in advance, if not sooner. Having plenty of time will ease the stress of packing and minimize the risk that you forget something essential. I recommend sorting your belongings into piles: things that must be taken, things that can be taken if you have room or you might want to bring later, things you'll leave in the US, things you can donate, things you can sell, and things that should simply be thrown away. Of the things in the must-take pile, subdivide them into things for your carry-on and things for your checked bag. This should help you pack the essential items, and make life easier at airport security.

Carry-On Items

- Only small amounts of liquid and gels may be carried on a flight. I recommend putting a few small bottles of shampoo and shower gel in your carry-on so you have something to use before you're able to find a local store.
- A lightweight and protective plastic folder or file to keep all of your most important documents, like transcripts and proof of acceptance to university.
- Keep copies of documents safe and secure at all times—pack them in your carry-on, in a hidden pocket if possible, separate from the original passport, credit cards, ATM cards, etc.
- Passport protector or wallet to keep your passport safe and cards secure. Stock your wallet with your student identity card, your traveler's insurance card, the credit

card and ATM card you'll be using abroad, a few dollars, and local currency if you have it. Empty your wallet of credit cards you won't be using or have been cancelled, and old business cards or membership cards.

- Digital cameras, cell phones (unlocked tri- or quad-band with appropriate SIM), web-cams, microphone for Internet calling, e-readers, and mp3 players, as well as their chargers and adaptors, should all go in your carry-on. You may want some of these items on the plane, and your cell phone and SIM card may come in handy as soon as you land. Take new electronic items out of their original packaging and use them to avoid import duties.

- You'll need at least one power adaptor (see below) in your carry-on so you can power up your cell phone or laptop immediately upon arrival.

- Guidebook on your host country or city. Carry on only if you need immediate access when you arrive (i.e. map).

- If you have a small translator or dictionary, you can look up any unfamiliar words right away. This strategy, at least from my experience, greatly increases your ability to learn the language, and can help you navigate your new surroundings immediately.

- A working laptop is essential for international calling, managing your bank accounts, watching American movies, doing your schoolwork, and much more. Your university may even require that you have a laptop. Again, take it out of its original packaging and use it a bit before you leave. If it looks new, keep the receipt of the laptop in a safe place to avoid having to pay duties on the way there, and to avoid customs duties when you return. While chances of being stopped are low, it is better to be prepared.

- Any prescription or other necessary medication needs to be packed in your carry-on in its *original bottle*. This includes contraceptive pills. It may also be necessary to include a doctor's note to pass through customs. Be sure to also bring glasses or contact lenses, and don't forget sunglasses.

- A journal to reflect upon your experiences as they occur, tape ticket stubs into, draw your first impressions.

Other Items to Consider

- **Backpack** (large, sturdy backpackers-style pack). Even if you don't plan to backpack while you're overseas, a backpack is fantastic while transporting your entire life to another country. It frees up both your hands to drag a suitcase and dig into your wallet for money. And you'd be surprised how much can actually fit into a medium or large pack. If you don't think you'll use it often, a cheaper version is probably fine. If you plan to travel every weekend and during academic vacations, you should consider a more expensive, durable version. Because good backpacks last for decades, you can find them used. Check Craigslist or Amazon before buying new.

- **Large roller bag.** If you don't already have decent roller luggage, you'll want to invest in a large roller bag for your move. You'll definitely want one that is relatively lightweight when empty, so that you can load it up as much as possible without exceeding the airline's weight limit. Again, if you're planning this move on a budget, be creative about finding used items before running out and buying new.

- **Carry-on bag.** You'll want a smaller bag as well for your carry-on luggage, and you can use this bag to take to school with you if it is big enough for a laptop and a few books.

- **Luggage tags and locks.** I recommend using sturdy plastic luggage tags rather than the flimsy paper tags you can get at the check-in desk for free. Even if you don't have a local address yet, you can write your name, phone number (if you pre-purchased a phone and SIM card or your US-based Skype number) and email address. If you buy luggage locks, make sure they conform with TSA guidelines; otherwise they'll be cut off. Luggage locks are also helpful if you plan on traveling and staying in hostels.

- **Power adaptors.** You'll need power adaptors for your electronic devices and other appliances you're bringing from the United States. Different regions of the world use electricity operating on different voltages, and any device plugged into the outlet needs to be able to run on that voltage. The two most common types of electricity are 110 and 220 volts. Fortunately, many newer devices such as cell phones, cameras, battery chargers, and laptops are all designed to work with either voltage. You can check whether your device will work overseas by looking at the battery pack ("the black brick") or looking at the documentation that came with the device. The battery will say 110-220v if it can work on either system. In this case, all you need are the plug adaptors, which are small devices that fit over the existing plug so that it will fit into the foreign outlet. Once you plug in the device with the adaptor attached, the device will automatically switch to the appropriate voltage. You'll need to find out the shape of the outlets in your host country so you know which type of adaptor to buy. It is important to buy these devices before you leave, because it may be difficult to find the right adaptors (compatible with American plugs) once you're overseas. You can find power adaptors at stores like RadioShack and BestBuy, and they're not very expensive.

- **Convertors and/or transformers.** If one of your devices won't work on the voltage in your new home, you'll need either a convertor or a transformer. In my experience, these tools work, but imperfectly. Before running out to buy a convertor or transformer, consider the appliances you're thinking about bringing with you. Keep in mind, any appliance you consider to be essential can probably be purchased abroad, and if you're renting a furnished apartment you may not even need to purchase anything at all. Hairdryers should be left at home because they don't tend to interact well with power convertors and end up causing power outages. You can find power convertors in specialty travel stores and stores like RadioShack. Sometimes, power convertors are designed with the appropriate plug shape to fit into the outlets overseas, but other times you'll need to also buy the adaptor as described above.

- **Climate-appropriate clothing.** If you're going to a climate that is vastly different from where you currently live, consider buying some clothing appropriate to the new climate. However, in this case, it is probably better to purchase the bulk of your new wardrobe after you arrive and you have a better idea of what the daily weather is like. Additionally, clothing may be a lot cheaper where you're going. Cut off the tags of any new clothing and wash them to make them look worn. Otherwise, customs officials might suspect that you're importing them for commercial purposes.

- **Comfortable walking shoes.** Break them in before you leave. You may be doing a lot more walking in your host country than you're used to.

General Tips

- **First aid kit.** I recommend putting together a very basic first aid kit so you'll have these things at your immediate disposal. The most basic health supplies should be available in most places around the world, but having a few things with you, especially while you get your bearings, can be very helpful. Your first aid kit may include over-the-counter painkillers, anti-diarrheal medication, antacids, Band-Aids, condoms, first-aid cream, tampons or sanitary napkins.

- **In-flight entertainment.** Think about what you'll need to keep yourself sane and entertained on the flight, and throughout your travels abroad. Most international flights have a decent in-flight entertainment program with several choices of movies, TV shows, radio stations, and even interactive games. If you want to watch your own movies, consider renting them on iTunes, or bring a good book.

- **Clothing.** The bulk of the space in your bags will be for clothing. Most of your clothing should probably be put in your checked baggage, but think about carrying on an extra shirt and pair of underwear for the first couple of days, in case your checked bags are delayed. What items of clothing you bring will ultimately depend on your destination and style.

- **A Piece of Home.** Although space in your bags will be limited, make room for something small that reminds of you home, such as a photo or keepsake.

What NOT to bring

I find that having a list of things not to bring helps focus on things *to* bring. Put a mental "X" on the following items and disregard them, no matter how tempting it might be to make room in your bag. Trust me, you won't need them and you'll feel happy that you didn't bring them.

- **Appliances.** Not only are they heavy and awkward to pack, they won't work abroad. Most appliances won't work with the different voltages other countries use. You'll most likely be moving into a place that has some kitchen appliances available to you, like a shared flat or on-campus housing. This includes other appliances like hair curlers and hairdryers. The only exception might be men's electric razors, many of which are designed to work internationally. Leave these things at home, or sell them if you won't be back for a number of years.

- **Furniture and household items.** This may seem obvious, but you won't need any furniture, pots or pans, rugs, drapes or anything in this general category. Even if you end up moving into an apartment that you will need to furnish, it will be easier and cheaper to do so once you arrive.

- **Food and drink.** Ok, I admit to packing a whole box of microwave macaroni-and-cheese packets when I first moved abroad, only to find out that my apartment didn't have a microwave. You won't know what a typical kitchen setup looks like in your host country. Generally, fruits, vegetables, meats and other perishables aren't allowed by customs regulations anyway. A few snack items for your carry-on to last you through a long plane ride are acceptable. Any edibles you bring should be lightweight and individually packaged. Remember that liquid won't be allowed through security.

- **Anything outside of customs regulations.** Know your host country's customs regulations. Customs officials are usually looking for commercial items (things intended to be sold in the host country), alcohol, cigarettes, luxury items like perfume, and certain food products. There may be specific items that are either strictly prohibited or will come with a rather expensive import duty. Leave such items out of your bags unless they are absolutely necessary.

- **Large amounts of cash.** Think you'll avoid that international wire fee and instead bring cash into the country? You'll be subject to expensive import duties on large amounts of cash, and having cash on you is risky. You'll make yourself a target for theft, as well as arouse suspicion by security officials.

- **Sheets, towels, and pillows.** These items take up a lot of space and together weigh a lot. Your sheets may not fit the bed you'll be sleeping in overseas, and again, if you're moving into a flat or subletting an apartment, they may be provided.

- **Books.** As a full-time student, you probably won't have time to read for leisure. And books weigh a lot. If you really want to take books with you, pick one or two and bring paperback versions or if you prefer, buy an electronic version. Go through all your books before you leave. Used books can be sold at books stores or on Amazon if you need extra money.

- **DVDs.** Maybe you think you'll want a few DVDs either for the plane or for those nights when you're looking for a taste of good old American cinema. Your DVDs from the US won't work in a player in other regions of the world. DVD players and DVDs come with "region codes" in order to protect against copyright infringement. DVDs can also arouse suspicion from customs agents who might suspect you of bringing in Hollywood movies to illegally pirate.

- **Formal or business clothes.** In your day-to-day life, you won't need formal attire. The student culture in most universities is casual. You may want to pack just one formal outfit in case you have an interview or want to dress nicely for a presentation.

- **Anything big and bulky.** When I was packing, for some reason I thought I couldn't live without my bathrobe. I tried to fit it into my bag many times, but decided to take it out in the end. I was able to use that space to pack a bunch of t-shirts instead. Similarly, you may have trouble packing a heavy sweater or jacket, but remember that these items can be worn on the plane.

- **Liquids.** Shampoo and body wash are also heavy, and you risk having them explode all over your clothes.

Arrival Plans

As your arrival date nears, begin to make arrangements for what you will do in the first couple of days. The first few days will likely feel chaotic, as you are confronted with initial impressions of your new surroundings, as well as all the administrative and bureaucratic necessities of making your home abroad. You can ease stress by planning.

Contact the university and ask for their recommendation regarding arrival steps. It is possible that the university offers an airport pickup service for international students. It is also possible that the university offers housing on a temporary basis while students look for permanent arrangements. Even if they don't offer these services, they may be able to give you some direction and advice on where to go and what to do once you've arrived. If you've made contact with some current students online, you can reach out to them for help as well. Perhaps one of them can offer to meet you at the airport, take you to campus, and assist you with your luggage. Even better, one of them may offer to let you stay in their apartment for the first few days while you get yourself oriented.

If you can't find someone to stay with and the university is no help, you may need to make reservations at a hotel or hostel. Make a reservation in advance, even if there is a chance you could end up canceling. You don't want to show up after a very long day of international travel and be turned away because they have no extra rooms.

Not only do you need to know where you'll be spending the first few nights when you arrive, but you'll need to know *how* exactly to get there. Ask the university or another contact how best to get from the airport to where you'll be staying. Find the city's public transport system online (if it exists and in English), and plug in your starting point and destination. You may even choose your hotel around public transport. If you'll have help with your luggage, a few transfers between busses or subway lines will be manageable but without assistance, you won't want to maneuver too many buses. You may opt for a taxi this first trip from the airport, but do some general research and get an idea of how much it costs. Additionally, plan your transportation around what time you'll be arriving. If you're arriving late at night, your only option might be a taxi, but you'll need enough local currency to pay the driver. Currency exchange counters may not be open at night and therefore you'll need to find an ATM to withdraw enough cash for a taxi, or find a taxi that accepts credit cards.

Arrange to meet up with a contact at the university within the first few days. This could be the head of your program, a representative of the international student office, a professor, or a student ambassador. This person will be able to tell you what to do next, answer any immediate questions you might have, and give you an idea of where to begin looking for accommodation. This will be the most pressing and difficult task to complete once you've landed overseas.

You can start looking for a place to live while you're still in the US. Talk to current students and ask them where they live, and where the cheaper safe neighborhoods are located. Perhaps there is an Internet-based search tool for apartments where you can begin. You can even arrange meetings with roommates and landlords over email.

9. Airports and Airplanes

"There are only two emotions on a plane: boredom and terror." —Orson Welles

So far on your journey to college abroad, you've said "yes." Yes to the option of college abroad, yes to the offer for admission, and yes to moving overseas. Now it's time to begin writing your story, and it starts at the airport. If you've never flown internationally before, this chapter will help to demystify international air travel. Although flying can be a bit stressful and confusing, knowing what to expect ahead of time will help make the experience more manageable.

Jet Lag

The severity of jet lag will depend on how much you slept on the plane, your point of origin, and your destination. If you're going to South America from the US, you probably won't experience much jet lag because you won't be going across multiple time zones. However, if you're traveling eastward or westward from the US, jet lag will increase the further you travel. If you cross the International Date Line, not only will the time of day change but the day of the week, too! Jet lag is worse if you're flying eastward because in order to adjust you have to go to bed earlier than usual, and this is more difficult than staying up late.

Familiarize yourself with the time difference between your old home and new home, and look at what time locally you're landing. If you make small adjustments to your sleeping schedule in the three to five days before you get on the plane, you can hopefully adjust faster and feel less tired. If you're traveling westward, try to force yourself to wake up one hour later and go to bed one hour later in the days leading up to your departure. Similarly, if you're going eastward, progressively wake up one hour earlier and go to bed one hour earlier.

Airport Arrival

If you purchased your airline ticket online, you'll probably receive a reminder of your flight via email at least 24 hours in advance. You can check in online from the carrier's website, but for an international flight you'll still have to go to the check-in counter to drop off your bags and have your passport inspected.

Plan how and when you'll get to the airport. The general rule for international travel is to arrive three hours before your flight, although in my experience this is more than enough time. When you get to the airport, immediately go to the check-in desk for your airline. If you're checking in a large backpack, ask the agents for a large plastic bag. The plastic bag keeps all the straps safely secured and reduces the likelihood of the bag being torn by the conveyor belts.

You might have the option to check in at a kiosk or with a human being. Either way works. The kiosk will ask you to scan your passport. It will then display your itinerary. Check to make sure the itinerary is correct, and make note of any schedule changes. It will then ask you about your seat selection and checked baggage. If you indicate that you'll be taking more than one piece of luggage, the kiosk will probably then tell you that you need to wait for assistance. You'll place your bags on the scale, and pay the extra fee for either going over the weight limit or for the extra bag. Your luggage should be checked through to your final destination, and in this case, you will not see it again until you get there. An agent may check your passport to assure it's not expiring within a certain required period (usually 3 to 6 months) and that you have the appropriate visa. Then you will receive a boarding pass as well as claim tickets for your checked bags. You'll probably receive all boarding passes for each of your connecting flights, so be careful to put them in a safe place.

Your next stop is airport security. Have your passport and boarding pass ready to be inspected by a TSA agent. You can prepare for the security screening by taking your liquids out of your bag as well as your electronic devices. Before you leave the security area, be sure you have your passport and boarding pass, your wallet, and all other valuable items.

Now you'll find your gate and wait for boarding. International flights tend to begin boarding one hour to 45 minutes prior to departure. Once you board, settle in and relax! Try to get some sleep if possible. The first few days of college abroad will inevitably be exciting and tense, and you'll want to be as alert as possible.

Flight Delays

Airlines do their best to schedule flights so that passengers have enough time to switch planes between flights. For long-haul international flights, layovers can be several hours. However, if your first flight is delayed and you have only a short time to get to your next flight, ask the flight attendant if you can disembark before the other passengers. I've seen this happen several times and the other passengers tend to oblige. Ask the flight attendant if he or she can find the gate number of your next flight so you can immediately walk (or run) there. Many airlines include maps of major airports in their on-board magazines. Once you know the gate number of your next flight, look at the map so you can know exactly where you're going.

If your layover is in another country, you may or may not have to go through passport control before boarding your next flight. Most airports have separate immigration for connecting flights, with less stringent security protocol. Unfortunately, there aren't too many options for speeding up this process. If you're only passing through the country, and have the appropriate transit visas, you'll probably get through passport control rather quickly.

If you arrive at your gate and you've missed your flight, remain calm and take a deep breath. Find a gate agent and ask what to do and where to go. There is usually a central desk where rebooking requests are handled. If the missed connection is the fault of the airline, they should assist you in rebooking. If the next possible flight is the next day, the airline should offer you a voucher for a hotel room and a meal. If weather caused delays, the airline should help you find another connection but may not offer you a hotel room. If you purchased your flight with a credit card that offers travel protection, you may be entitled to certain benefits from your credit card company. Be sure to keep your ticket stubs, receipt for a hotel stay and any other paperwork so you can claim these benefits. The same applies if you purchased travel insurance. If the missed flight is your fault, you may end up having to buy another ticket to your final destination if you don't have any of these protections. Be sure to ask the agent about your bags as well. Due to security regulations, bags that make it on a plane without an accompanying passenger have to be removed. Therefore, your bag should be waiting for you somewhere in the airport.

Customs and Immigration

Some countries require that paperwork be filled out in addition to presenting your passport and visa to immigration authorities (the United States is one of these countries and you'll be required to fill out a form when you return to the US). You'll probably be given the forms on the plane shortly before arrival. There may be different paperwork for different types of passengers, so be sure you're filling out the correct forms. These forms will probably request general information such as your name, address and phone number, as well as information about your travel plans. You may have to disclose the purpose for your voyage and the address of where you'll be staying. In addition, you may have to fill out customs forms explaining items you plan to declare.

If you already have a visa or you're arriving in a visa waiver country, the first line you'll enter is passport control, or immigration. If you're arriving in a country that requires a visa but one that can be acquired at the airport, the first line will be the line for the visa. You'll probably be asked to fill out a small form and pay a fee. Be sure to get in the correct line. Usually there are lines for specific nationalities and for local citizens. Present your passport and be prepared to also show your letter of admission if they ask. Although uncommon, you may have your picture or fingerprints taken (this is common practice for people entering the United States). The official may slide your passport through a computer to make sure you don't pop up on any security watch lists. He may ask you some basic questions like, "What are you doing here in _____?" or "What is your final destination?" Just answer honestly and don't be nervous.

After clearing immigration, you'll be directed to baggage claim. Wait patiently for your luggage and after collecting it, you'll pass through customs. Each country has different customs regulations, but usually things that fall under the category of "personal items" can be brought in without a problem or having to pay a duty. Personal items are things you will be using yourself. The form you filled out should have some general guidelines as to what you need to declare and what you do not. Should you need to declare something, fill out the form appropriately and be ready to take the item in question out of your bag for inspection. Most countries have a customs exemption, which means that you won't owe any duty on items below a certain value, provided they're not commercial goods or restricted. I've never needed to declare anything either in a foreign country or when returning to the US, but you can safeguard yourself by having receipts for electronics as well as doctors notes and prescriptions for the drugs you're carrying.

Give the agent your customs declaration form. If he wants to inspect anything, he'll ask you to open your bags. If you have to pay a duty on a certain item, you'll be directed to do so directly at a cashier's desk at the airport. They may accept US dollars, but you may have to get cash at an ATM to pay in local currency. In some countries, particularly in Europe, there will be two lines for customs. One "green" line and one "red." The green line is for passengers with nothing to declare, and the red to declare. Just because you choose to declare something doesn't mean you'll have to pay a duty on it, and if you walk through the "green" line you may still be asked by a customs official to open your bag.

113

10. Navigating the First Few Days

"There is no moment of delight in any pilgrimage like the beginning of it." —Charles Dudley Warner

Surely, you'll be full of excitement during your first few days of arrival. All things are new, but there are also a lot of rather mundane, administrative tasks to be handled within weeks of arriving. Be forewarned that tasks that may be easily accomplished within a few hours at home may take days or even weeks to complete in a foreign country. This is because things will be done differently in another country and because as a foreigner, you may have to go through extra steps.

You can alleviate much stress by arriving early and giving yourself lots of time to take care of logistical matters before the start of classes. Rely heavily on the advice of other international students who have gone through the process before, and ask the university what to do in order of priority. The university may provide a checklist of things to do, and may recommend specific people or places that have affiliations with the university or English-speaking personnel.

To save yourself hassle, be mindful of the order in which you do things. You may need health insurance before you can apply for a residence permit, and you may need a local bank account before you purchase health insurance. In my experience, sometimes there is an impossible circular logic inherent in these bureaucratic matters. For example, I was told by the insurance company that I needed a student ID to purchase my health insurance at the student rate, but I was told by the university that I needed to have a health insurance card before they would give me my student ID. As strange as this was, after several conversations with the relevant authorities, I was able to resolve the problem.

Jet Lag Adjustment

Jet lag can manifest itself in a variety of ways. Not only does it produce feelings of fatigue and lack of mental acuity, it can also cause irritability and an upset stomach. Combined with unfamiliar food and the challenges of intercultural communication, your first few days abroad may be particularly challenging.

Try to live the local time, no matter how tired you feel. If you arrive in the morning, stay up until the evening. Although it may be tempting to immediately go to sleep, this will throw your schedule off so much that it could take days, even weeks, to completely feel adjusted. One way to stay awake is to expose yourself to as much light as possible; this will send signals to your brain that it's daytime. Another good strategy is to expose yourself to external stimuli and remain lightly active.

On the other hand, if you arrive at night, try to sleep as soon as possible. If you're finding it difficult to fall asleep, do quiet relaxing activities like reading or meditating. Don't watch TV, as the light will trick your brain into thinking it's daytime. Don't drink caffeine either, and if hungry, eat healthy and light. If you can't fall asleep at a reasonable hour, set your alarm so that you'll wake and get up in the morning, even if that means only sleeping a few hours. This will help you adjust faster.

Illness

You might have heard horror stories of travelers becoming severely ill during their trip. It can happen, but it's not very common. What is common is to experience some sort of physical discomfort in the first few days of moving abroad. You can avoid many other health problems by reading up on the culture beforehand and knowing what to expect in terms of the water quality, the local cuisine, hygienic practices, the typical bathroom situation, and other common cultural practices.

Your body can adjust to new conditions if you ease yourself into it. Although it may be tempting to run out and try all the traditional cuisine and see all the popular tourist destinations, remember you are not a tourist, and you'll be able to experience everything you want at the right time. Even the slightest differences in food and water can do things to your body that you're not expecting. I seem to always have a mild stomachache for a few days after returning to either Europe or America, and I've come to accept it as a normal part of my body's adjustment.

If you feel sick, don't panic. Rest and drink lots of water, but be careful with the water. Even if the local water is perfectly potable, it may have additives (or lack thereof) that bother your system. The hardness or softness of the water may have similar effects. Therefore, drink bottled water for the first few days, and add tap water (if potable) little by little, allowing your body to adjust. Put off drinking alcohol until you feel better. Most illnesses are temporary. Try to think of them as a rather uncomfortable but necessary rite of passage.

Where to Live

If your housing wasn't pre-arranged and on-campus housing isn't an option, you'll need to find an apartment. This process will likely be the most challenging aspect of college abroad, besides passing your exams. Hopefully you were able to get some basic information ahead of time regarding how one goes about finding an apartment. Housing in some countries may be tightly regulated by the government and you may have to put your name on a waiting list; this is the case in Sweden. You may find a fully furnished apartment or you may need to furnish it yourself. You may also be required to pay a large security deposit upfront, with your first and last month's rent.

The university will probably guide you on where to start looking. There may be a list of landlords they've worked with in the past or a list of available apartments near campus. Students seeking roommates may also advertise with the university. There may also be specific groups or organizations that help expatriates find homes. Don't forget you can search wherever and however locals find their accommodation (website, classifieds, agent, etc.). Although sites like Craigslist have an international presence, most rental listings are for tourists, and are priced well above the going-rate.

You need to know the average cost for the type of housing you are seeking and what you can afford. It's a good idea to only view apartments in your price range. If you allow yourself to look at larger and more luxurious apartments beyond your means, you may be tempted to spend more than you should. Most students attempt to spend as little as possible while still feeling comfortable and safe in their homes. Keep in mind, you probably won't be spending lots of time at home, between classes and exploring your environment.

Be prepared for apartments that are smaller than what you're accustomed to, and with fewer amenities, even in developed countries. Student apartments in Europe don't typically have clothes dryers, microwaves, and dishwashers; they have small refrigerators or mini-kitchenettes. You should not expect large eat-in kitchens or common living rooms or even closets. Don't expect swimming pools or gyms, either, although these may be available at the university. The furniture may look and feel very different. Even the sheets may look different. As long as you're open-minded and realize this is the way that most people live, you'll probably get used to it very quickly.

Before you start searching, ask around if you can see the housing of current students, to better gauge affordability and location. Get to know other newly arriving students at orientation events as possible roommates. Don't be afraid to ask lots questions of landlords, even if they seem obtuse. Ask about security deposits, how and to whom one pays the rent, other expenses that come with the apartment such as cleaning and trash fees, whether TV and Internet are included and if not, how one goes about getting these services, what appliances and furniture are included, the type of heat the apartment uses and how much utilities are supposed to cost, where the nearest public transport stop is located, where the nearest grocery store is located, and what the neighborhood and neighbors are like.

Once you find the place you'd like to live, whether permanent or temporary, be careful about the lease. Before signing anything, make sure you read and understand everything. While you may have taken signing a lease for granted in the US, read the contract down to the last detail in a foreign country. If the lease is in a language that you don't understand, take it to a native speaker and confirm that there is nothing unusual or extraordinary. If there is anything that sounds strange, ask someone! You don't want to get stuck with a large unexpected bill at the end of the rental period that was clearly in the lease.

Be sure you understand when you're supposed to pay rent, how you're to pay (cash, check, electronic transfer, at the bank, online, etc.). Are bills handled at the post office? What do you need to do in order to get your deposit back? If there is anything at all that you're concerned about that isn't specifically written on the lease, ask the landlord about it (as well as any roommates) and have it written and signed by all concerned parties. Although this may feel overly cautious, remember that not only are you entering in a legally binding agreement, you're also dealing with an unfamiliar legal system and culture. When I lived in Budapest, I made a verbal agreement with my landlord to stay an extra month, but when that month came, she suddenly claimed she didn't understand the verbal agreement and she had a new tenant ready to move in. I'm not sure what happened, but if I had insisted on a written agreement, there wouldn't have been a problem.

As a foreigner, you may have to provide the rental agency or landlord with a copy of your visa or passport or proof of your ability to pay. Here's an example of when your acceptance letter from the university and documents from your bank or funding agency will come in handy.

Registration with Local Authorities

Although some may not require it, many countries require foreigners (and sometimes the local citizens as well) to register with the authorities. You'll probably need a local address in order to do this. Instructions for where to go and what you'll need to complete the registration will probably be provided to you by the university, but you can also consult the immigration office. Make sure you have all of the vital documents and information with you before heading to the office. You'll probably need your passport and visa, documentation from your funding source, proof of having health insurance, proof of having a local bank account, documentation from the university, and a copy of your lease agreement. Although you may be attending an English-speaking university or program, local bureaucrats may not speak English. Therefore, seek the advice of other international students and ask if it is advisable to bring a native speaker with you.

Foreign bureaucracies can seem like a psychological and physical maze. Don't expect the Monday through Friday, nine to five schedule that is fairly typical of government agencies in the US. Government offices close on public holidays, and many countries have quite a lot of holidays! Some countries have different workweeks; for example, throughout the Middle East the weekend is either on Thursday and Friday or Friday and Saturday. You may have to wait in long lines, too. The best thing to have is patience. The process may be slow, but there is no sense in getting upset or complaining, since it's not going to make the experience any more pleasant. When your registration is complete, you'll probably receive a number or card (similar to a Social Security Card in the US). Keep this card in a very safe place, as you may need it for things like getting your visa renewed or getting a job at the university.

Local Bank Account

You'll probably need a local bank account for day-to-day transactions. If possible, choose a bank that has a branch near your new home that gives you a decent interest rate. Although online banking may not be common in your country, it's always helpful if you can find a bank that offers that service. At the very least, you'll want an account that gives you an ATM card so you can access cash whenever you need it. Your student status may give you access to special rates or other perks, such as a free checking account. Ask the university and students about what bank and what types of accounts they recommend, as well as what documents you will need to set up an account. You'll probably need your passport, residence permit, local address, registration documents, and initial cash deposit. Bank personnel may not speak English well, so unless you're comfortable with the local language, ask specifically for someone who speaks English or take a native speaker.

Once you have a local bank account set up, you'll need to figure out how you're going to fund your account. If you'll be transferring money from the US, tell your local bank that you'll be receiving large international wires and ask them for the appropriate information. Then, call your bank back in the US to set up an international wire transfer, and remember that 1-800 numbers are free through Skype. You can also use third-party currency trading services such XE (www.xe.com). You'll need to give them the following information from the bank account into which you're transferring funds: the exact name of the bank, the bank identifier code (BIC), also called a SWIFT code in some locations, the IBAN number (international bank account number), the name on the account, the address of the bank (either the main office or the specific branch affiliated with your account), and the address associated with the account holder. Before completing the wire, make sure the bank in the US quotes you an exchange rate as well as any fees they'll charge you. The exchange rate they quote you will be slightly worse than the current going rate, because in addition to the fees, the bank makes money on the difference between the actual exchange rate and what they charge you (called the "spread."). An international wire usually takes 5-7 business days to show up in your account overseas, depending upon your host country. The US has passed laws monitoring overseas cash transfers, so international wires to certain locations may take more time.

Residence and Work Permits

Unlike a visa, which is obtained *before* entering a country, and gives you permission to enter for a particular purpose, residence permits give you permission to *stay* in that country on a semi-permanent basis. While a visa may not be required, a residence permit is necessary. A residence permit is often required before you can officially register for classes, open a bank account, and purchase health insurance. Usually, you have to obtain the permit within three months of arriving. Some property owners may require a permit of residence before they will rent their apartment to a foreign student.

You may have been required to get a residence permit from the embassy before arriving, or a "provisional" residence permit, in which case you'll need to convert it. The documents that you will typically need for a residence permit are similar to the visa. Be sure to bring everything you need with you to the immigration office, including payment for the fee. If you don't have everything you need, it could complicate the first few days of your stay. Follow the instructions carefully and try to have patience.

Once you have your permit, make a note of when it expires. Usually they are issued for one year, even if your program lasts longer. A few weeks before it expires you will have to go through the same process again to get it renewed. Don't let your permit expire. If you do, this may cause serious delays in getting it renewed, and you could face deportation! Your residence permit is your official, legal permission to stay in the country and shouldn't be taken for granted.

You probably checked with the embassy prior to arrival regarding whether you're allowed to work in your host country, and if so, what you need to do so legally. In some cases, you can work a limited amount of hours without a work permit. If you would like to work more, you'll need to apply for and obtain an additional work permit. The process to get a work permit will be similar to that of obtaining a residence permit, but will probably require even more documentation.

Health Insurance

Unless you're automatically enrolled in a national health plan, you'll need to choose a company and a plan, sign up, and pay for it. Again, ask around and confirm any information you found ahead of time with the university and other students. If you have a choice between companies and between public and private schemes, be sure to ask all kinds of questions about the differences in coverage. Don't simply choose a plan because it's cheaper. My international friends in Germany, who chose the private plan based solely on the price, ended up regretting their decision. The private schemes denied coverage for preexisting conditions, required payment for treatment upfront, and gave them the run-around when they tried to get reimbursed. On the other hand, the private insurance in Germany pays for some select treatments that the public does not, like acupuncture and chiropractic care. The private plans also allows for a few luxuries, such as private hospital rooms. Consider options carefully, with your budgetary and personal health care needs.

Once you've chosen a plan, enroll as soon as possible. I recommend doing this in person rather than over the phone, especially if you're communicating in a foreign language. Ask for an English-speaking representative or bring a native speaker to translate. The process may be as simple as filling out a form and arranging for payment. The form will probably ask you some personal questions about smoking, surgery, past pregnancies, etc. This is normal, even in the US, so just answer honestly. The company may require that you undergo a basic medical examination prior to being covered. Confirm how to pay for your coverage, how often to pay, and what you need to do when you go to the doctor. Will you be responsible for a co-payment? Is there a deductible? What paperwork do you need? What is the process for getting reimbursed? Do you have your choice of doctors or not?

When you get your insurance card, keep it in your wallet and always carry it with you. In addition to health insurance, you may be required (or recommended) to buy other kinds of insurance. For example, renters insurance can protect against inadvertent damage to your apartment for which you would otherwise be responsible.

Getting Around

You'll get to know your new home simply by wandering around between home and school. However, a local transport map or city map can really help you navigate in your first few days and weeks. This will also help you find your way to all the places we've discussed in this chapter: the insurance company, the bank, potential apartments, etc. Of course if you have a smart phone and Internet access, there may be an application for the public transport system or you can use Google maps while you get your bearings. Keep the maps with you at all times for easy reference. Consider purchasing a monthly or annual public transportation pass as soon as possible, if you'll be using it frequently to get around. Doing so will likely save a lot of money. It may be the case that your student fees include a transport ticket.

Student ID and Course Registration

Once you have legal permission to study in the country, you'll be able to get going as a student. The university should inform you of any necessary steps and deadlines. You will have to take care of a variety of logistics, which vary from school to school but may include the following:

- Fill out paperwork with your new local contact information and sign a document confirming your enrollment and agreeing to abide by the rules of behavior and academic honesty
- Pay tuition and/or fees (if any)
- Get your photograph taken in order to get your student ID card
- Visit the library to set up an account
- Review and sign additional agreements concerning the rules of the dormitories
- Pick up keys to the building and your room
- If you're a graduate student, you may also be issued keys to the library, to the laboratory, or to your on-campus office
- Get cards or personal identification codes that gives you access to certain buildings, copy machines, and printers on campus
- Get a personal email address, as well as a user ID and password for access to the Internet
- Get your laptop set up for use on campus
- Install some specific software to make full use of web-based applications the university uses

- Find out how many credit hours you are required to take per term, as well as the total credits needed to graduate
- Choose the classes you'll be taking and register
- Note, some programs, especially graduate programs, have pre-selected courses that all students in the program must take
- Find out if there is a sample period for classes, before you have to make a final decision regarding what courses to take for credit
- Purchase a meal plan, if you want to eat on campus, and ask questions about how it works

Be sure to familiarize yourself with the expectations for any classes you decide to take. Is there an attendance policy? Is it set by the professor or is it a university-wide policy? What should you do if you miss a class? Are you expected to actively participate in class discussions? Are you allowed to take notes on your laptop during class? Do the courses require you to purchase books or is the material available online? Will you be required to give in-class presentations? Can you take classes on a pass/fail basis or for participation credit as opposed to full credit? If you take classes without full credit, be sure you do not compromise your ability to complete the program on time.

The university may take you through an orientation for new students. You may be offered campus tours, meetings with current students and professors, and even off-campus events to help you feel more at home and get to know your colleagues. However, many international universities won't guide you in the same way US universities tend to do. You may need to take the first step rather than expecting them to offer you assistance. Most foreign universities tend to treat students as independent adults and expect them to navigate through the system with little assistance. They feel (rightfully so), that they are in the business of education, rather than stepping in and acting as a parental figure. It is simply a different cultural logic surrounding education.

If your college abroad takes a rather passive role in directing student responsibilities and activities, don't take that to mean that you're supposed to just know what to do automatically. Especially as a foreign student, you won't look foolish if you have questions. The offices that are responsible for areas of student life may be entirely different from what you'd assume to be the case at a US university. To be perfectly frank, the hierarchy and organizational logic of a foreign university may not make any sense to you at first. My advice is simply to ask someone, *anyone*, and if they don't know the answer, ask them where to go next. You may have to ask several people or go to several offices before you finally get what you need. Another way to really understand how the university is organized is to join a student-led government organization, which will require you to interface with various offices and administrators.

11. Living in Another Country

"There are no foreign lands. It is the traveler only who is foreign." —Robert Louis Stevenson

Culture Shock

Culture shock, despite the name, isn't actually shocking. The things that may shock you about a culture are things like seeing an entire pig's head, raw and bloody, for sale at the local market, or the way in which people will literally stand on top of each other in the city buses. These are things that are so radically different from what you would normally see in the US that you can't help but be a little shocked, even if you know about them ahead of time. Most shocks wear off quickly. Either you rapidly train yourself to avoid that section at the market or the sight of the pig head becomes part of your weekly routine.

Rather, culture shock presents itself slowly and in stages over time. Initially, it may be as simple as small misunderstandings, such as people never being on time, saying no when they mean yes, or suddenly realizing that real Thai food tastes completely different from the *Som Tam* you are used to getting at home. These are the things you will likely experience in the first few days and weeks after moving abroad, similar to what most people experience when they undergo a radical change of environment.

Real culture shock is the gradual but eventually overwhelming realization that even the most familiar things aren't

127

as familiar as you thought. It takes a certain amount of insight into the local culture, beyond superficial observations, to really experience culture shock. It is the disorientation that comes with knowing that despite your best efforts to integrate, you are still viewed as an outsider and you may never be completely accepted. It isn't shocking because you may not even realize what you're going through. It requires deep reflection, a change of routine, and a reevaluation of yourself, your priorities, and how you relate to others, to alleviate the symptoms.

Everyone experiences culture shock differently. You may feel silly, stupid or childish because you can't figure out how to execute the easiest of procedures. You may feel caught between your struggle to fit in and act like a local, while retaining your sense of identity. You may feel sadness, homesickness, alienation, confusion, and even hostility and anger. You may find yourself adopting opinions about yourself and the US that you otherwise wouldn't have. Perhaps the most difficult part is not being able to talk to anyone about what you're feeling. Local friends can't relate to what you're going through and may even react defensively if you point out things you don't like about their culture. Friends and family can make you even more homesick and may lead to a blind idealization of life back home. While other Americans in your area probably understand what you're going through, conversations can quickly turn into an unintentional cycle of reconfirming and exaggerating negative stereotypes of the local culture.

Clinging to stereotypes and gravitating towards fellow Americans is a natural reaction to culture shock, but these strategies are not very effective and will likely prolong the symptoms. There isn't a simple remedy that works for everyone, but it is important to realize that while uncomfortable and difficult, going through culture shock is normal and necessary. Even if you speak the language, are well traveled, feel generally happy about your decision to go abroad, and are successful in school, you will still feel culture shock at some point in time. You're not a bad, uncultured or close-minded person when you experience culture shock, even if it shows itself with distinct enmity. It is how you handle culture shock that makes you a better and more cultured person.

When you're dealing with the worst and deepest mani-festations of culture shock, one of the best ways to feel better is to take time for yourself. Be a tourist for a day; go to the local attractions you have not already seen. When you go to a tour-isty place, you don't have to worry about standing out or saying the wrong thing, since it's expected. Plus, you can see some-thing that is important and unique to the local culture, while reflecting on the perspective and history of your surroundings. It serves as a reminder of why you came in the first place and allows you to focus on what is interesting and positive about your new home and its people.

It is important to realize that culture shock is a problem with *you*, not with the culture. Although there may be aspects of the culture you reasonably do not like or disagree with, culture shock isn't about what is wrong with the culture, it is about carving out a space within it where you can find balance between being yourself and growing from your surroundings. There are appropriate times to challenge or discuss the truly negative aspects of the culture, but deep moments of culture shock are not the right times to do so. This is because you're simply not in the right frame of mind to have a reasoned and balanced conversation about what you find disconcerting or unintelligible about the way local people live or behave.

Getting through culture shock is not about uncritically accepting the culture; it is about understanding and appreciat-ing a culture, for better or worse. It is about adopting a healthy, balanced and educated opinion about the cultural practices of a given people. In this sense, while culture shock is difficult, it is also an essential learning curve. It is usually a good sign when you're going through culture shock, since it means that you're engaging in your environment beyond the obvious and your perspective is moving along a path of discovery. When culture shock is over, you'll better understand why people behave the way they do (even if you don't like it).

Another strategy is to change your daily routine. Carve out time to go to your favorite café to read a good book or take a walk in the park. Mild physical exercise rejuvenates the body and mind, making it easier to focus on what you like about your new home rather than the things you don't like. Getting out is crucial—staying at home and withdrawing from society will make things worse. Try to include one thing you love about the local culture in your daily routine and another thing that reminds you of home. Wander through your favorite neighborhood or shopping district in the morning and watch your favorite American movie with some salty popcorn (if you can find it!) in the evening. Getting through culture shock is about finding balance between your home and host culture.

Once you feel you have gotten at least partly through the most tumultuous and reactionary phases, you can then reach out to your local friends and ask them to include you in their outings and ask them questions about the culture to help you better understand. Tell them about a certain cultural practice that makes you feel uncomfortable and ask them if they have any insights. Approach discussions with curiosity and a genuine desire to understand, rather than attack or diminish. Go out with your American friends as well and discuss your newly discovered logic of the culture, resisting attempts to demonize it.

Culture shock passes with time if you take positive steps to mitigate it. You'll eventually get to a place where you feel generally happy about your life and where you live again, with a new appreciation. Some experts in the field of intercultural communication call this phase "integration acceptance." It can take years to reach a place where you are an accepted, integrated local, and in fact, it may never completely happen. I've known several people who grew up in Germany, speak German flawlessly but still feel as if they will never be accepted as German because they're not ethnically German and they'll never adopt all the automatic signs and symbols that define a culture. This isn't a bad thing; in fact, being "glocal" (a person with a lot of local knowledge but with a global or outsider's perspective) is quite liberating and makes you a noteworthy addition to the country.

If you live abroad for a number of years, culture shock is a repetitious cycle—with several periods of isolation followed by periods of fascination and adjustment. In this way, culture shock is never completely "over." Every time you go through the alienation phase, you'll learn something new about the culture and how you fit in. Each bout of depression will be slightly different from the last and your coping mechanisms will change, too. Remember, culture shock is a growth and learning process. When you first graduated from arithmetic to calculus, you probably had an initial period in which this new type of math was foreign and frustrating. But at some juncture something clicked—and you got it! You may not become a Nobel Prize-winning mathematician, but the knowledge attained and the ability to do something you couldn't do before is incredibly rewarding. If you approach culture shock this way, you'll get through it more easily and with a deeper and more informed perspective, with each passing phase.

Health Concerns

First, add emergency numbers to the contacts in your phone. While there is probably something equivalent to "911," there may be other phone numbers for requesting an ambulance, directory assistance, or English-speaking help. Depending upon your grasp of the language, you may want to try to find an English-speaking doctor who accepts your insurance. Your insurance may reimburse you for taxi fare to the doctor, or house calls for example, but only if you follow proper procedures. Depending upon your insurance plan, be prepared to pay for treatment upfront or a co-payment when you visit the doctor. Understand how far in advance you need an appointment, or if you can simply walk in. Know what to do if you need medical assistance during unusual hours, such as late at night or on weekends. You may be allowed to go directly to a specialist or you may have to get a referral first.

The treatment options available in your host country may be different from what you'd expect or what you've experienced at home. Be open-minded and don't assume the treatment is inferior just because it may look and feel different. Health care may be more holistic in its approach, and doctors may not as readily prescribe drugs compared to doctors in the United States. While I think it is important to engage with the local health system and be open to different types of treatment options, in some situations you might want to seek "Western" treatment, especially for very serious or personal scenarios. In such situations, American consulates normally keep a database of doctors and facilities in the host country.

In the case of an emergency, don't hesitate to go to the hospital right away. If possible, bring with you your medical biography. After getting to know your fellow students and making some close friends, include the contact information of someone locally on your medical bio sheet and ask the doctor to contact that person if you have to go to the hospital. It can be very comforting if you're facing a serious medical problem to have someone familiar nearby. Ask for a translator if you feel that you're not able to communicate clearly with the doctors. Even in countries where you would normally have to wait for treatment, you should be admitted to a hospital right away if your symptoms are serious.

The availability of medications that in the United States are over-the-counter may not be over-the-counter in your host country. Don't immediately assume that you can just find the nearest pharmacy and buy what you need. Ask your doctor about pharmacies and the general policy on obtaining certain medications. Delivery service may also be available for pre-scription medications.

Become acquainted with your university's policy regarding health conditions and schoolwork. Certain conditions may not be grounds for missing class or assignments, but you may be permitted a certain amount of free "sick" days each semester. If you have to get proof from the doctor in order to be given leniency on attendance and assignments, you should be aware of this ahead of time and be prepared to ask the doctor when you see him/her.

If you're a woman, and you did your research ahead of time, you should at least be prepared for what a woman faces regarding reproductive health care. Know that it's quite common to experience late or even missed periods when a woman moves abroad, due to the combination of jet lag, shift in diet, and stress. Some countries have excellent health care for women, even exceeding what is generally available in the US, but some countries will probably fall below your standards. If you're in a country where women face discrimination, finding a female doctor may be difficult but not necessarily impossible. If you have to see a male doctor but don't feel comfortable, ask to have a female friend or female nurse in the room with you at all times. If contraceptives are difficult to obtain in your host country, keep a supply of condoms.

The US Embassy's list of recommended physicians is helpful, as well as the database of medical providers through the International Association for Medical Assistance to Travelers (www.iamat.org). If certain services are difficult to obtain from a local physician, look for a provider of gynecological exams and family-planning services through International Planned Parenthood (www.ippf.org).

Dating

Dating across cultures is challenging, as two often very different people attempt to read the codes of what is both said and unsaid, while risking embarrassment, misunderstanding, and the possibility of severely hurt feelings. However, navigating the cultural codes of flirting and dating is one of the most illuminating processes a person can go through in another country. It allows you to take part in customs that you would otherwise not experience, and get to know someone outside your own cultural space on a very serious and personal level. The process by which this happens will give you a nuanced and sophisticated appreciation of the culture and language.

Of course, having a decent grasp on the language is one of the first windows into any culture's dating world. There may not even be a word that can be accurately translated as "dating." While it is helpful, language fluency isn't a requirement to date abroad. Learning a new language from someone you care about and trust is one of the best motivations and gives you access to phrases you won't learn by taking traditional language classes. Being intimately involved with someone from another country and culture brings together a multitude of complex cross-cultural, multi-generational, and multi-linguistic dialogues, both spoken and unspoken.

You'll probably make several observations right away. Do men and women go out together or is public life somewhat segregated? Do they hold hands or kiss in public? Are many of your classmates married? Do women dress modestly in public? When you go out with friends from school, where do they go? Do they appear to flirt? How quickly do they have intimate relations with new people they meet? Is it appropriate for a woman to ask a man to get a coffee? Observe the behavior of friends that are in relationships. Do they act physically toward each other at all? What is the level of commitment they express towards each other? How long have they been together and how did they meet?

Perhaps the first step when it comes to dating and flirting abroad is knowing how to unabashedly say "no." In some cultures, "no" either means "yes" or "maybe." In patriarchal cultures, men don't expect women to refuse their advances. You should know the verbal and non-verbal signals to get the message across. If you feel uncomfortable or threatened, you have every right to leave cultural sensitivity aside and react in whatever way will ensure your safety. You can further protect yourself by going out with trusted friends, staying in groups, keeping a charged cell phone on you, knowing where you're going in advance, knowing how you'll get home, and keeping the amount of alcohol that you drink to a reasonable level.

Dress appropriately according to cultural norms so as not to give anyone the wrong idea. Of course, you don't have to dress *exactly* like a local (such as donning certain religious or national garb), but observe the limitations and don't stretch them too much. Don't bring someone home with you until you really feel comfortable you're both on the same page. Be very prepared and know how to practice safe sex. If you insist on using a condom and your partner refuses, don't be afraid to hold your line. If you don't plan on having sex, be very honest about this and gauge the person's reaction. If you refuse or reject someone, be cautious as you go home and make sure that no one is following you. Although you will have to make some concessions in your approach to people, you shouldn't engage in a relationship that feels disrespectful for the sake of cultural sensitivity.

Don't be afraid to ask local friends if you didn't understand something that was said to you or something that someone did, during what you understood as a flirtatious encounter. Ask them for advice on how to continue with the relationship. Be open with your "interest" about the dating expectations in your own culture. Intercultural relationships have to find a balance between both cultures; you don't have to accept all of the rules of your host culture in your personal life. If you're interested in dating someone abroad, being in a university environment is one of the most fruitful places to begin a relationship as you're surrounded by people in your general age range with similar interests and potential career paths. However, if you're interested in getting out of the campus bubble, ask friends where they would go if they were looking to meet new people.

The dating scene for gay, lesbian and bisexual expatriates may be even more complicated due not only to cultural nuances but also to how homosexuality is perceived. Don't be openly flirtatious if you haven't quite grasped the local perception of homosexuality. Perhaps there are different expectations for how a gay or lesbian individual fends off unwanted attention than there are for a heterosexual person. And of course don't sacrifice your own sense of safety in the pursuit of integration, go out in groups, practice safe sex, but remain open-minded to meeting new people and the possibility of starting a new relationship.

Personal Safety

The best way to stay safe is to be less like a tourist, less like a foreigner, and more like a local. Fortunately, the more you find your way in your new home, the safer you'll probably become. There are no other secret rules to staying safe abroad that are different from what you should do at home. Know areas of town to avoid, become more familiar with the city to avoid getting lost, and know how to read people and sense if a situation is becoming dangerous. The key is to find a balance between excessive paranoia and passive naivety.

Know the location of the nearest police station and hospital, and don't be afraid to go there. Be vigilant about your drink when you're at a bar and don't drink it if you have any reason to suspect that someone has tampered with it. Don't wear expensive jewelry out in public. Remember that foreign universities may not have "campuses" in one central location and therefore may not have dedicated campus security guards. Familiarize yourself with safety recommendations and procedures if you were the victim of a crime. To be very cautious, put extra money in a secret location such as another pocket in your wallet, in case of an emergency. Know what forms of identification foreign residents are required to carry. Some countries require you to have your passport with you at all times, other countries advise you to keep your passport in a safe place at home while carrying a local form of ID with you. Always have some sort of ID whenever you leave the house. The good news is, unlike a tourist, you'll have contacts nearby that you can rely on in case of an emergency. If your wallet or passport gets stolen, you can go directly to your bank and request a new ATM card, and if your passport is stolen, you won't face a time crunch in terms of getting it replaced before you fly home.

That being said, crime can happen to anyone, anywhere. My wallet and passport were stolen while living in Germany. In fact, it happened on the bus line I had taken every day for two years. This is the most common type of crime you're likely to experience—petty theft. The rule for dealing with theft is the same as it would be at home. If you're being threatened with physical harm, just give up your wallet without a fight. However, you don't have to be threatened to be robbed. Oftentimes, pickpockets find a clever way to get your wallet without your noticing. That is what happened to me. If you discover your wallet is gone, go to the police as soon as possible and file a police report. They probably won't be able to recover your belongings, but a report alerts police to pickpocket tactics and having a report will help you replace your passport and credit cards. You should tell the appropriate person at the university what happened. They can advise you on whether further steps are necessary. If you need a translator or require more assistance than the police are willing to give you, contact the nearest US Embassy or Consulate. Although their power is limited, they can advise you on the local criminal justice system and can help you get a lawyer if you need one.

Of course, more serious things can happen, too. Tens of thousands of study abroad students were recalled from their programs in the Middle East during the wave of revolutions in 2011, and from Japan after the earthquake and subsequent nuclear meltdown. Natural disasters and political upheaval are a small but real risk no matter where you go. You'll need to rely on your college abroad and your own good instincts to help you in case of a serious problem. If the political situation becomes unstable, avoid public demonstrations and get to a safe place. Try your best to get to the US Embassy, where they can give you a safe-haven and advise you on your options for possible evacuation. If you purchased optional travel insurance, it may include evacuation funds. Other resources include the International Red Cross and local rescue workers, in severe situations. Notify friends and family back home regarding your status, if possible. They can contact the State Department regarding what the US government is doing to help what steps if any, either you or they should take.

Theft

If your credit or ATM cards are stolen, call the companies and banks to cancel the cards. Go to the university to replace your student ID. Then you will need to patiently wait for the new cards. Most US credit card companies will send a replacement card to your international address.

Losing your passport is an urgent matter. A passport is your official international identification. It contains your visa and residence permit. Without a passport, you can't travel and you won't have any proof that you're in the country legally. If your passport is lost or stolen, there are detailed instructions for what to do on the State Department's website. The process is relatively painless (and I know from experience). You'll get along much easier if you have a copy of the passport as well as a police report if the passport was stolen. There is a central 1-800 number to invalidate your passport and begin the process of getting a new one. You'll have to fill out several forms and pay a fee in person at the US Embassy or Consulate. While you wait for the new one to arrive, the embassy can provide you with a legal document that recognizes your US citizenship. Of course, you can't travel with it. If you have a trip scheduled that would be difficult and costly to cancel, you can request that the process be expedited, but you'll pay a higher fee.

Once you get your passport, you'll have to go back to the local authorities to request another visa. If you have copies of your original permit you'll be in a better position to get a new one. You might need to pay another fee and complete forms.

137

Voting

I've actually been quite surprised to find that Americans abroad are not aware of their right to vote. If you register with the Overseas Vote Foundation, they can send you alerts well ahead of an election in your district to remind you about the deadlines for both local and federal elections, and to request an absentee ballot. They can also help you fill out the proper paperwork and give you the correct address of your local county clerk. You'll need to complete a Federal Post Card Application to start the overseas voting process. Some districts are even equipped to accept registration and ballots via email, making the process even easier from abroad. Information and forms are also available at any US Embassy or Consulate. It is important to complete a new Federal Post Card every year and whenever you change address.

Legal Problems

It is your responsibility to know the local laws. Although it would be impossible to know every single law in your host country, those that are of particular importance to travelers and foreigners will be noted in most guidebooks. You have very little recourse if you are charged with or found guilty of a crime other than what the local justice system affords you. The rights you enjoy as a US citizen at home don't travel with you abroad. As a non-citizen in your host country you may not have all the same rights as local citizens either. Some basic information on local laws is also noted on the State Department website. If you are ever faced with a situation where you are unsure of the legality of an activity, always err on the safe side. Ignorance is no defense. Penalties for what would be a petty crime in the US may be severe overseas, and the right to legal representation may not be the norm. Furthermore, violating local laws can be grounds for expulsion from your university and maybe even deportation from the country. If you use common sense and become a keen observer of your surroundings, you'll be able to avoid legal trouble.

Perhaps the most common violation American students commit abroad is public intoxication and noise. The "fraternity" or "spring break" culture common to American universities isn't so common abroad, and the lower drinking age in many countries outside the US can be very seductive. As a college abroad student, you'll be entirely responsible for your own decisions and actions. It is perfectly within your right to drink if local law permits. However, doing so excessively brings down your usual guard and makes you especially vulnerable to crime. Being publicly intoxicated can carry serious penalties abroad, even in countries with low drinking ages. My advice is to avoid heavy drinking in general, but especially during the first few weeks of living abroad. Take this time to get to know local students and observe their behavior and what they do for fun on the weekends. Also, get to know the city, campus, subway, and bus lines that take you home at night.

The use of drugs abroad poses similar safety issues as excessive alcohol use, with perhaps much stronger legal consequences. While drinking within limits is legal and even an acceptable social norm in many countries, drug use often is not. Simple possession can carry extreme penalties, so avoid this potential disaster. Even if some drugs, such as marijuana, are legal, it is probably best to avoid taking any drugs while overseas. It is difficult to know which drugs are legal and which aren't, how much you're allowed to have and whether you're only allowed to do so under certain circumstances.

If you face legal trouble, the US Embassy can visit you in jail and provide some basic assistance in finding you an attorney. They can act as a liaison between you and your family at home, and make sure you're being treated within the bounds of local as well as international law. However, the US government will not typically intervene on your behalf and cannot provide you with legal representation or financial assistance. Therefore, the best way to handle legal concerns abroad is to avoid problems in the first place. Be respectful of local customs and laws, become informed, and err on the side of caution.

Classroom Culture

Classroom culture will vary, depending upon the type and size of the university, the country's cultural understanding of higher education, the international population of the university, the working language of the university, and the type of degree you're pursuing. It will be difficult to know what to expect before you're actually sitting in the classroom, but you can look for syllabi of previous classes posted online and read through the requirements.

In my experience, respect for deadlines varies dramatically by culture. While deadlines are relatively strict at US universities, they may be more flexible abroad. There might be a university-wide policy regarding assignment deadlines and how late one is allowed to turn something in, as well as the penalties for doing so. Or it could be that each professor is allowed to make his or her own rules. Similarly, while a class is supposed to officially start at 9 am, you may arrive to an empty classroom then. This relates to cultural conceptions of time and is part of the learning curve in adapting to a new culture. You'll quickly learn what time classes start effectively.

Once you figure out what time classes really start, you may find yourself in a huge hall with several hundred other students, in which the professor lectures for the entire class. Attendance may be taken and required or completely voluntary. The professor may make little effort to know the students and will simply deliver the required material according to a predetermined syllabus. Your job is to show up and take notes, do the required outside reading, and pass the final exam.

Classes may also be discussion-oriented rather than delivered via lecture. In this case, they may be somewhat smaller and the professor will know the students on a more personal level. Rather than simply giving a lecture, the professor will lead a discussion in which students are expected to participate. However, knowing when and how to participate, how to do so effectively, and within the cultural expectations, will take time. In America, we're taught to be assertive and even sometimes competitive in the classroom, and that we should not hesitate to offer our ideas and thoughts. The same rules could apply to your classroom discussions abroad but the parameters may also be different.

Individuality is not as highly valued in some places as it is in the US. Therefore discussions may be less about expressing your personal character and "outsmarting" your colleagues, and more about coming to a consensus-oriented understanding of the text in question. While it would be considered rude to interrupt the professor or another student in the US, this may be par for the course in another learning culture. What may seem like a heated argument in the US may be how normal classroom discussions proceed overseas. Part of knowing what to do, and when to do it in the classroom, will require some personal reflection as well as some adjustment. It is a stereotype of Americans that we tend to dominate conversations and depending upon your personality, you may have to teach yourself to hold back in the classroom and make room for others. If you're in a very diverse classroom, you'll want to be culturally sensitive to others' style of participation. Pay attention to the syllabi of every class you take and know what is expected of you.

It is likely that you'll have to write a research paper at some point during your college abroad experience. Writing a paper is a difficult task, let alone doing so in a culturally unfamiliar environment and perhaps in a non-native language. If you're unsure what a good research paper looks like, ask the professor if s/he can provide you with a sample essay that would earn a high grade. Make a note of the structure of the sample. Even if it isn't a normal custom at your university, ask if you can make an appointment with your professor to discuss in detail the expectations of a lengthy research paper. Note the citation style that is preferred by the university or the specific professor. Some cultures may take page or word counts very seriously while others universities may take these as mere suggestions. If you're writing in a foreign language, make use of any resources available to have your worked edited or proofread by a native speaker.

Don't get frustrated if your first major piece of academic work is not as successful as you might have expected. You'll be dealing with what may be a steep learning curve not only with regards to academics, but also in terms of cultural and personal learning. Step back and try to evaluate whether a less than perfect grade is the result of not fully understanding the cultural expectations of quality academic work, or whether you truly didn't live up to the standards. You have the right to ask the professor what you did wrong and how you can improve your work in the future. Remember that some professors may not have much experience with foreign students and while it wouldn't be right to discriminate, your writing style may sound strange or awkward to them. Know your rights as a student in protesting against an unfair grade, but do so cautiously and reflectively. And remind yourself that grades aren't everything. If you get a less than stellar grade on one essay, it is just one small hurdle. Take it as a learning experience and try to improve the next time.

Of course, as a PhD student you may not have to take classes at all. Your work is making progress on your dissertation and attending regular meetings with your supervisor. You may be required to *teach* classes, in which case you'll have to adapt your teaching style to the culture of the university, even if that doesn't comport with your natural instincts. When I taught my first class as a PhD student in Germany, I took it for granted that students would know how to engage in a lively class discussion on topics related to the required reading. I forgot that my students were undergraduates, and some of them were in their first year of college and had no idea what I meant by class participation. I also took it for granted that they would have some basic knowledge of the topic and when I discovered that the department had not listed any prerequisites for my class, I had to rewrite the syllabus overnight. If you're teaching a class for your professor, work closely with him or her so that you know what they would do and wouldn't do in class. Make sure you understand the university's rules and regulations regarding what is expected of teachers and the rights and responsibilities you have in that capacity. Be friendly and open to criticisms from students.

Foreign Grading System

Most study abroad programs, unless self-designed, will already have a system in place for converting your credits and grades completed abroad into the American system in such a way that your home university recognizes your efforts. However, if you go to college abroad you'll most likely be receiving grades according to the national system. You'll need to understand what a grade *means* in your host country and what you need to do in order to earn a high grade. This is important not only for achieving your highest academic potential but also for translating your achievements to universities and employers at home. Many foreign grading systems include a much broader range of possible grades than the A-F scale that the US uses. Furthermore, many countries don't have a problem with grade inflation, like the US, meaning it is more difficult to achieve the highest possible grades, and an "average" grade (a "C" in the US) isn't considered all that bad.

Every country has its own grading system, although there have been some efforts towards harmonizing grade scales on a more international basis. The Bologna Process is perhaps the widest attempt to integrate the structure of higher education across states. Currently, there are over 40 signatories to the initiative ranging from the United Kingdom and much of continental Europe, all the way to Turkey and even Kazakhstan. The goal is to make it easier for students and employees to move across borders by standardizing degrees, grades, and credits. Although the US isn't part of this scheme, the structure created by Bologna borrows a number of features from the US, and is designed in part to make a degree from any member country easily transferable to the US. Members of the Bologna Process are at different stages of implementing the changes, which could mean that your college abroad may offer degrees from both the traditional system as well as BA, MA or PhD degrees under the Bologna Process.

If your college abroad happens to be a Bologna member, the process of understanding the local grading system and how to "translate" it into the American scale is rather straightforward. The Bologna Process created a grade scale and credit arrangement called the European Credit Transfer and Accumulation System, or ECTS. Universities under the Bologna system will not only provide a grade from the national grading system, but also the equivalent grade from the ECTS system. The Bologna Process then provides a framework for understanding what an ECTS grade would mean in the American context (as well as a variety of other national systems outside of Bologna). For example, if you were attending the Universidad Politécnica de Madrid, and you earned a grade of 7,5 (the Spanish grading system uses a numerical grading scale in which 10 is the best and 1 is the worst), it wouldn't be appropriate to simply assume that a 7,5 out of 10 is the same as 75%, which in the

American system would be a grade of "C." A 7,5 in the Spanish system is considered a "B" in the ECTS scale, and an ECTS "B" translates to an American "B+." According to the grade conversion provided by the World Education Service (www.wes.org), ECTS grades are equivalent to the following US grades:

ECTS Grade	Description	US Grade
A	EXCELLENT— outstanding performance with minor errors.	A
B	VERY GOOD— above average with some errors	B+
C	GOOD—generally sound work with notable errors	B
D	STATISFACTORY— below average with significant errors	C+
E	SUFFICIENT— meets the minimum standards	C
FX	FAIL—some work needs to be completed for credit to be awarded	D/F
F	FAIL—considerable work needed for credit to awarded	F

These conversions are simply for reference and your university may have its own conversion scale from ECTS to the US system. There is no "official" conversion to the US system to which every university under Bologna must adhere. But it can help you to understand how your grades abroad translate to a system you're more familiar with.

If you're attending a college abroad that is an "American-style" university, or is an overseas campus of an American university, grades may be given according to the US system. These types of colleges abroad may also give two grades, one from the US system and one from the national or ECTS system. Due to the fact that their mission is to serve a very diverse student population, "international" universities will probably be more equipped to deal with the convergence of multiple grading systems. Therefore, they will be more prepared to deliver your final scores in such a way that you can take them with you back to the US. Furthermore, countries that send many students to the US (like India and China) will also probably be ready to translate their grades to the American scale.

Colleges abroad that are not working under the Bologna Process may require some extra effort to understand and to translate back to the US. If the university doesn't already have a conversion scale, as well as a diploma supplement to explain the scale, you'll need to ask them to create one. It isn't enough to simply translate a local grade scale directly to the American system, as evidenced by the Spanish example above. Instead, one needs to study the frequency distribution of grades between systems in order to create a fair comparison. Based on national averages (or averages among the same type of school), one needs to compare, for example, the grade that would be awarded to the top 10%, top 25%, all the way down to the bottom 10% of students for each country. For example, if the Dutch grade of "8" is awarded to the top 15-25% of students, this would probably translate to a B+ or A- in the American letter system, because the top 15-25% of American students are awarded these grades. Still, a proper conversion would also include a brief explanation of the philosophy behind the grading system, including not only the lowest and highest grades possible, but also the distribution of these grades, the intervals in the scale, and the cut-off point between passing and failing. On a grade scale where 1 is the lowest and 20 is the highest, whole numbers (1, 2, 3...) may be the intervals between grades, while a scale of 1 to 5 might include intervals of one-tenths such as 2.3 or 3.7.

Although the grading system at your college abroad may feel strange at first, you will get used to it after only a short time. If your marks aren't as high as you might have expected them to be, it is probably because the highest grades in some systems are almost never given, as opposed to the US system in which A's are rather common. The US system is multi-tiered and students need high grades to be competitive, while in other systems, higher education is more streamlined and high grades aren't as important. However, if you feel you've been graded unfairly, ask for a detailed explanation of what criteria need to be fulfilled in order for a certain grade to be achieved from the administration.

You also have to convert your foreign grades into a US-style cumulative grade point average, and your university may already be able to do this for you. There are also companies that you can pay to convert foreign grades into a GPA recognizable to a US institution, such as the aforementioned World Education Service. However, you can do it yourself by making a few simple calculations. First calculate each class's quality point. To do this, you need to know the numerical value of each grade you received. In the US, this is done by assigning a numerical value to the letter grades. Typically, an "A" is given 4 points, a "B+" equals 3.3 points, a "C" is 2 points, etc. Therefore, to know the numerical value of a grade, you would first need to know the equivalent American letter grade. For example, the German scale uses numbers 1-5 where 1 is the best and 5 is the worst. To arrive at a class's quality point, multiply the American numerical value of the grade you received with the credit hours of the class. For example, I received a grade of 2.0 for a class that was worth 7.5 credit hours. According to the university, a grade of 2.0 is equal to a B+, with an American value of 3.3. The quality point for this class would be 3.3 multiplied by 7.5, which is 24.75. Do this for every class you took. Finally, to calculate your cumulative GPA you would then divide the total quality points achieved by the total number of credit hours taken. See the chart below as an example of converting German grades in a one-year program to a US-style GPA.

		1st Term	2nd Term	Total
Class A	Grade	1,33	2,7	
	US Grade	A	B-	
	US Value	4.0	2.7	
	Credit Hours	7.5	7.5	
	Quality Points	**30**	**20.25**	
Class B	Grade	3,33	2,33	
	US Grade	C	B	
	US Value	2.0	3.0	
	Credit Hours	7.5	7.5	
	Quality Points	**15**	**22.5**	
Class C	Grade	3,0	2,0	
	US Grade	C+	B+	
	US Value	2.33	3.33	
	Credit Hours	7.5	7.5	
	Quality Points	**17.475**	**24.975**	
Class D	Grade	1,0	3,7	
	US Grade	A+	C-	
	US Value	4.33	1.67	
	Credit Hours	7.5	7.5	
	Quality Points	**32.475**	**12.525**	
TOTAL CREDIT HOURS		**30**	**30**	**60**
TOTAL QUALITY POINTS		**94.95**	**80.25**	**175.2**
GPA				**2.92**

Packages and Visitors

Since you will be staying abroad for a number of years, there will probably come a time when you'll want a care package from home or even a visit from a friend or relative. As someone who has gone through the process of getting a passport, a visa, and traveling to your new home, you'll be in a unique position to advise friends of what to do in order to come visit you. With some knowledge of the language and attractions off the beaten tourist trail, you'll also be a perfect tour guide to visitors. Of course, visitors need to be aware of the fact that you're not a tourist and you'll have a potentially busy schedule with classes. Therefore, try to schedule a visit when you have a break from classes. Also, it is better to receive visitors after you've had some time to settle. If you are lucky enough to have someone come all the way around the world to see you, take it as an opportunity to visit places in your host country you wouldn't go to by yourself. Get out of the university town and see more of the country.

If sending packages, make sure you have your friends or family read through the customs regulations so they don't send anything that is prohibited. Sending packages, especially large boxes overseas is expensive, and often the postage will exceed the value of the contents. Depending on the country, there may be custom fees to receive the package, so beware. Items that are subject to duty are the responsibility of the recipient—i.e. *you*. This fee can be very expensive so make sure your friends and family are aware of this and only send small inexpensive items. Remember, the more stuff you accumulate, the more difficult it will be to move back home, so material items should be kept to a minimum. Finally, international shipments take quite a long time to arrive, so if your family is trying to get you a present in time for a birthday or holiday, they should send it in plenty of time. Family and friends can purchase electronic gift certificates on sites such as iTunes and Amazon, which don't require shipping and can give you access to American movies, TV shows, and eBooks. Family can also deposit money in your account at home and you can withdraw it using your US ATM card.

148

Clubs and Sports

Your college abroad is unlikely to have large organized sporting events. This is one of the trade-offs that you have to consider when going to college abroad. If you want to play college-level competitive sports, going abroad is probably not a viable option for you. However, your college abroad may have "club" sports that are much less competitive but open to a larger group of participants. In Berlin, my university offered quite a few sports organized as classes, ranging from basketball to kayaking. These activities weren't competitive and more about simply getting out of the classroom and being active. This was a great opportunity to do sports without the pressure of having to perform well and to meet new people. Your college abroad might have a similar set-up or it may not have sports at all. In the case of the latter, you can join a league organized by the city or join a local gym. Finally, if your school doesn't offer an activity that interests you, start your own! There may be funding available for such an endeavor, and this is an opportunity to bring some of your personality and culture to your college abroad.

The same may be true of clubs. There may be a whole host of clubs to join at your college abroad, or student organizations off-campus. Joining a club is a great way to meet new people with whom you have something in common. And even though it may not be common on your campus for students to start their own clubs, that doesn't mean that it is impossible. Start a club around an activity or a cause you believe in, or start an overseas chapter of an organization you're a member of back home. If there isn't already an international student club, this would be a perfect opportunity for you to share your unique perspective with the local students, and to create a close-knit community with other international students. This is also a great occasion to help the university to better serve future international students and recruit more students from abroad.

12. After College Abroad

"People travel to faraway places to watch, in fascination, the kind of people they ignore at home." — Dagobert Runes

Reverse Culture Shock

Should you decide to go back to the US, it's likely that you'll experience culture shock again. Even if you feel ready and excited to go back to the US, you will still go through some emotions upon reentry. Reverse culture shock will feel much different than the difficulties you faced when moving abroad. When you first go abroad, you may not know exactly what to expect, but you know that you're about to be surrounded by the unfamiliar. However, when you return to the US, you're probably expecting the opposite—that everything will be easy and familiar.

Unlike a short-term study abroad program, things probably will have changed back home while you were overseas for several years. It is easy to have a picture in your head of life back home based on what it was like when you left. Friends may have moved, married, or had children. Parents and loved ones may have changed jobs or retired. And beyond your circle of friends, the country may have changed. Perhaps there is a new president, a new social trend you're unaware of, or a popular new TV series that you've never even heard of. When your expectation of familiarity collides with the reality of change, it can be even more confusing and alienating than the original shock of going abroad.

Your opinion of the United States and American culture will have changed. This doesn't mean that you've become unpatriotic; it just means that your understanding of the US has become more refined and subtle. You'll be aware of the good and bad, both as a native and a foreigner. In this sense, you'll have a "four-dimensional" view of the United States. If you express critical opinions, people may assume you're being unpatriotic and they may have no idea how to react to your views. If you express a positive attitude toward your host country, people may also be unsympathetic, especially if your experiences in your host country don't fit with their stereotypes. You may be very excited to share stories and pictures of your experiences, and while some may be interested, others may not show the enthusiasm you expect from them.

All of this can lead to intense feelings of separation, depression, frustration and even boredom. Reverse culture shock can be worse if accompanied by physical symptoms such as drastic jet lag and dietary adjustments. There is no way to avoid some forms of reverse culture shock, but I can give you some advice that I've learned during extended stays back home. First, try to treat moving home the same way you treated your host country when you first moved. You were open-minded and you took in all the strange and beautiful things of your host country, and you noticed the small things that locals take for granted. Approach the US with the same wide-eyed and open attitude. Absorb the subtleties of how people interact with one another, why certain systems are the way they are, and approach these things with curiosity. Rather than dismissing details as unimportant or familiar, reflect upon them as if you were a foreigner. Resist the temptation to compare countries. Instead, try to understand why people are the way they are, independent of what you have grown accustomed to.

While there will be things that you're aware of that you missed (like buttery movie-theater style popcorn in my case), you'll notice things about the US that you didn't appreciate before. For example, I love the fact that you can go to a restaurant in the US and the server will smile and treat you with a friendly face. Before living in Germany, where servers aren't as friendly, I never really valued the feeling of going out to dinner and having good service. Appreciate things that work well in the US. Just as you found charm in unconventional places in your host country, such as the busy and dirty outdoor market, don't forget that similar aesthetics exist in the US as well. The assumption that you're completely familiar with your home county can blind you to these small moments of beauty.

Similarly, you'll notice things you don't like about the US that didn't really bother you before. For example, whether it is actually true or not, when I'm in the US I just feel like people talk *really* loudly and sometimes it just grates on my nerves. This has led me to seek out quiet conversations with my closest friends and find solitary places to just "be." Other ways to deal with this aspect of reentry is to reach out to friends in your host country. If possible, invite some of them to visit you in the US. Seek out friends in the US that have traveled or studied abroad and process your emotions by bouncing your thoughts off them. Join or start a foreign language club so you can keep up your skills and get to know others with similar interests as you. Watch movies from your host country and ask friends and family to watch with you so they can get a better idea of what your life was like. While it may be tempting to schedule your next trip abroad to escape reverse culture shock, try to get through the worse of it before going abroad again. You need to find that "sweet spot" between your life abroad and your life in the US, and doing so will go a long way towards curing culture shock and lessening the symptoms the next time you go abroad. Finally, once you've learned how to bring your life abroad and your US life into balance, you may think about a career that gives you the opportunity to express these insights or continue to travel.

Market your Experience

When it comes time to get a job, keep in mind that you're not just competing with Americans. You're competing with other students who have lived, worked and studied in numerous countries, speak *numerous* languages, have fascinating personal biographies, have done internships with the UN and the World Health Organization, and are incredibly smart, motivated and reflective. Whether you go for a career that is truly international or something more traditional, it is important to recognize the skills that living abroad has instilled in you and make those skills work in your favor. When you begin putting together job applications and updating your resume, think about how you can integrate your experience of living abroad into the story you want employers to know about you. While your resume should certainly include the degree you obtained, extracurricular activities in which you participated, and any jobs you had while in school, you should also include the unconventional skills that set you apart. Living abroad shows a definitive ability to negotiate challenging situations and the ability to adapt quickly and easily. It develops independence, maturity, problem-solving skills, communication, compassion, responsibility, as well as a deep sense of self-awareness.

Perhaps you acted informally or voluntarily as an English-tutor for non-native speakers while you were abroad. Although you didn't do this in any official capacity, it still shows that you have teaching skills, cultural competence, the ability to work well with a diverse group of people, and that your English skills are above average. Speaking English well is actually a valuable skill for many employers, especially if the job involves public speaking or writing. Perhaps you kept a blog of your experiences while you were living abroad. You can also sell this "hobby" as something valuable to an employer by demonstrating your creative writing skills, your familiarity with social networking platforms, and your advertising skills. Similarly, if you took a lot of photographs of your life abroad, you can use this as a demonstration of your creativity and perhaps even marketing ability. Perhaps you took some particularly interesting courses during your studies, courses that wouldn't be available at schools in the US. Even if the subject of the course doesn't relate to the job directly, it demonstrates unconventional knowledge and a proven willingness to learn. Even if the job you're applying to doesn't require foreign language skills, keep this on your resume! Speaking a foreign language demonstrates open-mindedness, the ability to learn a precise skill, cultural awareness, and a grasp of how to effectively communicate with people who have different learning styles, even among other English speakers. Moreover, with rapid globalization, you never know when a company suddenly needs someone with international experience or foreign language skills.

Think creatively about other "soft skills" that you improved while living abroad. If you completed a bachelor's degree in three or even two years, you can sell this as evidence of your hard-working attitude, as well as your exceptional time and stress management skills. Think about including any papers you wrote that required interviews, data collection, statistical analysis, media analysis, research from primary sources, the use of web-based resources or archives, interpretation of legal documents or anything else in the research process that would be valuable to an employer. If you participated in any large-scale group projects during your studies, such as working with a research group, a joint research paper, or a presentation, you can use that to prove you work well in teams and you have public speaking and presentation skills. Finally, just the act of going to college abroad shows a willingness to think outside the box and approach situations creatively. If you can't find a place on your resume to put some of these skills, make sure to include them in your cover letter and during the interview.

Graduate School

In the academic year 2009-2010, almost 300,000 international graduate students entered US higher education programs. It stands to reason that quite a few of these students received their undergraduate degree in their home country. If these students are able to get into graduate school in the US, there is no reason to think that having a degree from a foreign country will hinder your chances of doing the same. In fact, depending upon the field in which you plan to get your advanced degree, having spent significant time abroad may make you a more attractive candidate. For example, if you plan to go to graduate school for Eastern European history and literature, having lived in Prague or Budapest for several years and being able to speak an Eastern European language would certainly look good to any US graduate school. Furthermore, many graduate schools strongly encourage their students to do field research, and what better way to convince your program to pay for your research in Hungary than demonstrating existing cultural and language competency.

Discover the Possibilities

I remember when I graduated from Knox College and was facing the "real" world for the first time, and feeling very anxious. I had student loans to pay, credit card debt, and I still wasn't completely sure what I wanted to do with my life. When I graduated from my MA program in Germany, I had similar feelings of anxiety, but for different reasons. Although it had only been two years, I felt like I had a new life in a new country. I didn't feel like my international education was over.

For some, living overseas is a valuable experience but once it is over, they're more than ready to return to Hollywood films that aren't dubbed, fluffy pancakes with maple syrup on Sunday mornings, and conversations with friends at normal hours of the day. Others will build a deep emotional connection to their home away from home, and will feel as though they belong abroad. And still others will be conflicted; they will feel a need to go home to the people they miss but aren't fully prepared to leave the people they've become close to overseas. While anxiety and excitement are normal feelings when finishing school, these emotions will probably be more intense and complex if you attend school abroad. As your program ends, you'll want to reflect on how you've changed and whether those changes have affected your vision of how you want to live your life.

Perhaps you imagined going abroad and immediately returning home to work in your parents' business; now, you've fallen in love with the language of your college abroad, and you want to work as a translator in your host country. Perhaps you imagined finding work with a favorite organization abroad; now, you want to bring some of the culture and cuisine back with you to the US by opening up a restaurant serving your new favorite dishes. Perhaps you're in a serious relationship with someone you've met abroad, and you want to find a way to stay together. Perhaps you've become fluent enough in the local language that you can enroll in another program offered in that language. Perhaps you're ready to move on from your current country but living abroad has inspired a love of travel and you want to make your home in yet another foreign country. Living abroad is almost always a life-changing experience and whatever plans you had before entering college abroad may be radically different after completing your degree. It is not unusual to want to find a way to combine your American life with your life overseas. Not only will you be faced with the same decisions most college graduates must face, like whether to find work or continue with one's education, but you'll also be faced with the question of *where* to make these next moves.

If you want to find a job abroad, you'll need to do some research regarding the regulations for foreigners wishing to work. As a graduate from a local university, you may be given a "free" period of time after graduation in which your visa remains valid and you can look for work. This is the case in several European countries. You may be required to get a new visa that permits full-time work, and getting such a visa may require you to have actually gotten a job first. In many countries, a company must "sponsor" the application of a foreigner for a working permit. Sometimes, countries with a particular labor demand will give working permits to foreigners who fit the needed criteria somewhat readily, but if you're looking for a job in a sector that is overcrowded with applicants, getting a working visa may be difficult. Finally, you may be required to return to the US first and apply for the new visa from there. You'll also want to familiarize yourself with working conditions and other requirements for living and working abroad full time, such as minimum income and tax rates. Visit your university's career services center for help with applying to jobs locally. Not only will they be able to guide you through the necessary steps to apply for a job and maybe assist you with visa issues, they may even have a relationship with local employers seeking to hire new graduates. Make sure that if you plan to stay abroad, you don't let your visa expire before making the proper arrangements.

If you decide that you want to return to the US, either for school or to begin the job search, there will be a number of things you'll need to take care of before heading home. First, you'll want to talk with some of your professors and ask them if they're willing to be a reference. Establishing this relationship before you've left the country will make things easier. Be sure to get back any monetary deposits you made, like keys to a campus office or your apartment. If you have money loaded onto a prepaid SIM card or to a cafeteria card, either use up the difference, get the remaining balance in cash, or sell the card to another student. If you purchased furniture or other items you won't be bringing back, see if you can sell them to another incoming student. Be sure to get your diploma and, if necessary, any accompanying documentation such as grade translations or certificates of accreditation. You'll have to close your bank accounts, notify the health insurance company and any other entities which send you bills, complete check-out papers with the university, and perhaps you'll be required to notify local authorities that you're leaving the country. Exchange local currency into dollars before leaving the country, especially if it isn't commonly traded. Your bank in the US may not be able to change Norwegian kroner or Israeli shekels, but banks abroad can most likely trade their currency into dollars. Begin searching for your flight home early so you're not stuck paying for an expensive ticket. Finally, take a few days to spend time with the friends you've made abroad. Go out to eat, have a few drinks and let them know you're going to miss them. Make a plan with them for how you'll keep in touch after you leave.

And finally, other options that might appeal to you after you've completed study abroad are to look for international opportunities. If you don't feel the pressure to jump into the job market immediately, you could consider going abroad as a volunteer. Although I have not personally pursued this possibility, I know many who have. There are innumerable organizations that accept applicants to participate in volunteer projects abroad. Some of them charge quite a large fee to do so, while others charge only a minimal fee and provide modest housing and board for free. Volunteering abroad isn't limited to teaching English, although this is a widely available option. You can find something that works well with what you studied, such as projects involving health care delivery if you studied biology or pre-med, or something involving sustainable water treatment facilities if you studied environmental science or chemistry. One volunteer organization highly recommended by friends and colleagues of mine is WWOOF (World Wide Opportunities on Organic Farms). Volunteers work on sustainable farms all over the world, and in exchange are offered free room and board. The Social and Environmental Volunteer Exchange Network (SEVEN), www.the7interchange.com, is like an online classified page for volunteer opportunities around the world that may interest the college abroad graduate on a budget.

You may simply want to travel. Your language and intercultural skills learned during school will have given you the capability to do an extended backpacking trip. Thousands of people embark on long journeys with no particular itinerary and only a vague vision of where they plan to go every day. There are many blogs out there dedicated to this subject, as well as books. I'm a frequent reader of the BootsnAll Indie Travel Guide (www.bootsnall.com) and Matador Abroad (www.matadornetwork.com).

Positions with the United Nations or the Peace Corps combine deep cultural exchange, travel, and work. Peace Corps volunteers aren't traditional volunteers—they get health care while abroad, a small monthly living stipend, language training, and a rather generous reentry allowance once the project is completed. Volunteering with the Peace Corps is a competitive endeavor but as a college abroad graduate, you'll be among the more prepared of all the applicants. Similarly, the United Nations has jobs as well as volunteer opportunities across sectors in almost every corner of the world. Again, these positions are extremely competitive, but certainly not impossible to get. Prior experience abroad as well as language skills will give you an edge.

Finally, pay it forward. I hope your college abroad experience helped you grow in ways you never imagined, and you want to bring those experiences to others. Whether in an official or unofficial capacity, do what you can to help others study abroad, do college abroad, travel internationally, or learn a language. There are thousands of campuses in the United States that have international student offices and study abroad offices that need people with personal experience in these areas. There are universities all over the world that are seeking to bring more Americans to their campus. The field of international education is vast. You can do this without being paid for it—start a local international travel club, blog your experience, approach universities whose international student service is lacking, write a book. This book has been my effort to pay it forward. I hope it has inspired curiosity in the world beyond the borders of the US, and has made that world feel more accessible. As you close this book, I hope you feel empowered enough to embark on less traveled paths, and turn your life's script into a real journey. Write your own story: "Yes, and..."

CPSIA information can be obtained
at www.ICGtesting.com
Printed in the USA
BVHW040543191020
591291BV00014B/468

9 780972 132893